|THE AMERICAN PURITANS SERIES|

DIRECTIONS FOR A CANDIDATE OF THE MINISTRY

THE
AMERICAN
PURITANS

DIRECTIONS
for a
CANDIDATE of the MINISTRY

— COTTON MATHER —

Edited by Nate Pickowicz

PETERBOROUGH

H&E
Publishing

Directions for a Candidate of the Ministry
Copyright © 2021 by Nate Pickowicz

Published by: H&E Publishing, Peterborough, Canada
www.hesedandemet.com

All rights reserved. No part of this book may be reproduced in any form without written permission from the author.

Source in public domain: Cotton Mather, *Manuductio ad ministerium. Directions for a candidate of the ministry.: Wherein, first, a right foundation is laid for his future improvement; and, then, rules are offered for such a management of his academical & preparatory studies; and thereupon, for such a conduct after his appearance in the world; as may render his a skilful and useful minister of the Gospel.* Boston, Printed for Thomas Hancock, 1726.

Paperback ISBN: 978-1-989174-30-2
Ebook ISBN: 978-1-989174-31-9

Contents

The American Puritans Series ix
Introduction xi
Foreword xv

Directions for a Candidate of the Ministry

1. Death Realized 3
2. The True End of Life 7
3. Regeneration Essential to a Good Preacher 19
4. A Zeal to Do Good 25
5. The Right End of Studies 29
6. Study of the Languages 33
7. Study of the Sciences 39
8. Poetry & Style 45
9. Natural Philosophy 53
10. Mathematics 59
11. Study and Use of History 65
12. Some Useful Proposals to Students 79
13. Sentiments which Ministry is to be undertaken 83
14. The Manner of Reading the Scriptures 89
15. Studying a Body of Divinity 93
16. The Pulpit and its Glorious Work 99
17. Employments for a Vigilant Pastor 117
18. The Genuine Temperament of a Minister 127
19. Rules of Health 141
20. Rules & Maxims of Prudence 149

This volume is dedicated to
Dr. Owen Strachan
a tireless champion of
pastor-theologians everywhere

THE AMERICAN PURITANS SERIES

Over the last fifty years there has been a renewed interest in the Puritans. In past generations, works by the English Divines sat dusty and derided, but soon found new life through the efforts of D. Martyn Lloyd-Jones, the Banner of Truth Trust, Reformation Heritage, and others. Today, many of the once-forgotten Puritans are household names in the Christian community—men like William Perkins (1558-1602), Richard Sibbes (1577-1635), Thomas Watson (c. 1620-1686), Samuel Rutherford (1600-1661), Richard Baxter (1615-1691), John Owen (1616-1683), John Bunyan (1628-1688), Matthew Henry (1662-1714), and others.

However, during the Great Migration (1630-1640), not a few Puritan leaders fled persecution and made their way across the Atlantic Ocean to settle in the American Colonies. These early American Christian leaders were not only pillars in the church, but also acted as spiritual and intellectual fathers of a great nation. But many of these faithful pastors are relatively unknown, their work is barely read, and their publications have long been out of print.

The American Puritans Series exists to reintroduce the work of these first Christian leaders to a modern audience. Each reprint will consist of the author's original work, yet gently edited and modernized for the ease of the reader. By the grace of God, this series will help rekindle a love for the writings of the Puritans whose theology was built on the biblical doctrines of the Reformation. May a whole new generation see Christ afresh through the work of our spiritual ancestors.

Nate Pickowicz
Series Editor

Introduction

Nate Pickowicz

Cotton Mather was born to Increase Mather and Maria Cotton on February 12, 1663 in Boston, Massachusetts. Descending from two founding giants, John Cotton (1585–1652) and Richard Mather (1596–1669), Cotton would have quite the legacy to live up to, but he would not fail to meet the challenge. At age 11, he became the youngest student in history admitted to Harvard, where, naturally gifted with a prodigious intellect, young Cotton excelled at reading, writing, memorization, and recall. Such a gifting led him into studying theology, homiletics, church history, classic literature, science, astronomy, and practically anything else he could get his hands on! When his appetite for knowledge became insatiable, he ventured out into other languages such as Greek, Hebrew, French, and Latin.

After graduating from Harvard with a Bachelor of Arts degree at age fifteen, followed by a Master of Arts degree at age eighteen, Cotton soon began to feel a call toward ministry. While initially content to live in his father's towering shadow, the opportunity soon arose for Cotton to minister alongside him as a pastoral equal. Increase, a seemingly cold and distant man, initially balked at the notion of co-laboring with his son, but capitulated when the congregation of North Church in

Boston voiced their overwhelming support of Cotton. He remained as a minister in Boston until his death in 1728.

Mather was a pastor-scholar par excellence. Unlike his reclusive father, he engaged in a very public ministry, visiting church members, praying with the sick, and catechizing children. In addition to his pastoral presence, it is estimated that Cotton wrote more than 450 books in his lifetime. The scope of his writing is broad, and includes works of theology, such as *The Everlasting Gospel of Justification* (1699); practical works of piety, *Bonifacius*, or *Essays to Do Good* (1710); the first science textbook written in America, *The Christian Philosopher* (1720); works of history, his magnum opus—*Magnalia Christi Americana* (1702); he even composed a 4,500-page Bible commentary, *Biblia Americana* (1693-1728), which has only begun to be published in the twenty-first century.

In his commitment to Christian ministry, Cotton devoted himself to piety and faithfulness, and took it upon himself to pass the torch to younger ministers coming up behind him. Perry Miller notes that Cotton "had lived much, and he knew what had to be said to the clergy of New England were they to succeed where he failed."[1] And so, in his twilight years, he again took up his pen.

Manuductio ad Ministerium

In 1726, just two years prior to his death, Cotton published *Manuductio ad Ministerium*, or *Directions for a Candidate of the Ministry*. Considered to be "a last will and testament of New England's most ranging intellect,"[2] *Manuductio* represented

---

[1] Perry Miller, *The New England Mind: From Colony to Province* (Cambridge: The Belknap Press, 1953), 417.

[2] Miller, *New England Mind*, 418.

the culmination of Cotton's ministry wisdom to be imparted to the next generation. At a time when New England ministers were growing lazy in their labors, Cotton exhorts his readers toward pastoral and academic excellence. So impactful was the work, in fact, that Jonathan Edwards cited *Manuductio* as an inspiration and model for his own ministry.[3]

From the outset, Cotton's care for the minister himself is evident. He implores the reader to consider his own life in light of eternity, and to take seriously the call and duties of pastoral ministry. He singles out the minister's own spiritual condition as an essential component; he must not only be a saved and regenerated man, and devoted to holiness and goodness. Though it may be said that Cotton projects something of himself onto the would-be minister, in that, he insists he must be a scholar and a seeker of knowledge (he spends nearly half of his chapters discussing academic study); he also seeks to take the young minister under his wing, comforting him and exhorting him to be watchful even of his temperament, health, and relationships. There can be no question that *Manuductio* establishes Cotton Mather as a pastor of pastors.

On the use of Latin

Cotton frequently thought and wrote in Latin; it has been said that Latin was almost more comfortable for him than English. For this publication, I have chosen to leave Latin phrases in the body of the text in italics. Professor Barry

---

[3] Kevin J. Vanhoozer and Owen Strachan, *The Pastor as Public Theologian: Reclaiming a Lost Vision* (Grand Rapids: Baker Academic, 2015), 85.

DIRECTIONS FOR A CANDIDATE OF THE MINISTRY

Hofstetter has provided the translation in the footnotes, as well as additional comments when necessary.

Foreword

John Ryland

To the Gentlemen, and other several Christians, in London and the Country, who have the cause of Christ, and the honor of the Christian ministry at heart.

The office of the Christian Ministry, rightly understood, is the most honorable and important that any man in the whole world can sustain; and it will be one of the wonders and employments of eternity, to consider the reasons, why the wisdom and goodness of God assigned this office to imperfect and guilty man!

It is an office and character that are deeply interested in the highest concerns of God's perfections and glory. It is an employment that obliges a man to the closest attention, to find out the true mind of God in the Holy Scriptures. It is a work in which we are called, to instruct the minds of men in the noblest knowledge, and teach them to adore and love God. The great design and intention of the office of a Christian preacher are: to restore the throne and dominion of God in the souls of men; to display in the most lively colors, and to proclaim in the clearest language, the wonderful perfections, offices, and grace of the Son of God; and to attract the souls of men into a state of everlasting friendship with Him.

It is an office and work, the grand design of which is to turn the sons and daughters of Adam from darkness to light, from guilt to pardon, from corruption to holiness, and from ruin to eternal happiness. It is an employment that, when finished with wisdom and faithfulness, will be crowned with higher honors than were ever bestowed on the best kinds, and most renowned heroes, and most celebrated philosophers.

It is a work which an angel might wish for, as an honor to his character, yea, an office which every angel in heaven might covet to be employed in for a thousand years to come.

It is such an honorable, important, and useful office, that if a man be put into it by God, and made faithful and successful through life, he may look down with disdain upon a crown, and shed a tear of pity on the brightest monarch on earth.

It is a work that, when a man is called to it by the providence and grace of God, should be entered upon with fear and trembling. It should be approached with a mixture of terror and joy, of awful reverence, and holy pleasure. No man should dare to rush into it, *uncalled* by God, or unqualified by the gifts and grace of the Holy Spirit.

There are requisite to this office, an enlightened mind, a renewed heart, very tender affections; a fervent love to the souls of men; a fixed attention to, and delight in, the holy Scriptures, and a peculiar love to Christ; an ability to speak in proper instructive words; a firmness of mind, to resist all opposition; and the utmost care to preserve a good moral character in the church and the world.

To all the above qualifications, it is necessary and of great importance, that young men, before they enter upon the full work of it, should have a very considerable length of time to be separated from all the business and cares of the world, and in a great measure from the conversation and company of most Christians too; in order to acquire a habit of thinking closely;

FOREWORD

to exercise themselves in contemplation and prayer; to converse much with God, and their own hearts; to study the sacred Scriptures in the original languages with the utmost diligence and attention; and, especially, to improve by them in a way of devotional exercise.

For want of this useful and necessary preparation, many young men of promising gifts have been pushed too soon into public and stated work; and what has been the consequence? The churches know the consequence; but the young person themselves have most severely felt the fruits of these hasty proceedings; they have, to their cost and pungent sorrow, felt the loss to the end of life.

On the other hand, there may be an extreme likewise; not in the length of time allotted for their preparatory studies, but in the misapplication of that time; or wasting too much of it in studies, that have no tendency to form a solid and judicious minister of the gospel.

Certainly, everything should be made subservient to Divinity; and the best hours of every day, from the first moment to the last, should be employed in gaining, by close attention and prayer, a masterly knowledge of all the great doctrines of the gospel, and the richest methods of improving them in a practical and devotional manner. And if this be done to purpose, be assured, sirs, there will be no time for trifling in the space of four, five, or six years. This is the highest work, and the noblest employment of a young student; and if he has the strong, the capacious mind of an Owen, a Charnock, or a Witsius, he will find full work for it, not only in the course of his studies, but all the days of his life.

The scarcity of serious and evangelical ministers of every denomination, has been long complained of. If the Lord should remove a few of our ages and useful fathers, their loss will be most severely felt. The places of good and useful servants of God, are not soon filled up; an able minister of the New Testament is not formed in a day or a year; no, not in seven or ten years. Happy is that young man who arrives to any degree of maturity and strength of mind in the compass of twenty years! I am sure it is worth twenty years study to be able to state clearly and defend and improve practically the truths of our holy religion. I dare affirm that I have the concurring sentiments of all those who are the best able to judge in this matter.

If these things are true, then how careful and zealous ought we to be to encourage and assist all young men in our churches who appear to be endued, not only with grace, but gifts for the ministry; or shall we sit still and say, "The Lord Jesus will provide (by a miracle) for all the wants of His people and churches, and there is no need to use any means at all?" But, my friends, does He do so in providence for your bodies and families? Did He give you all your wealth, and trade, and spacious houses, by a miracle?

Does He act thus in His dispensation of grace in order to your growth in knowledge, and holiness, and the comforts of religion? Are you not obliged to use diligently all the means of grace, and constantly too, in order to have the comforts of grace?

Now ought serious Christians to use time and pains to grow in knowledge and grace; and have not ministers, who are to preach the great truths of God every week to many thousands of immortal souls; have they not need of all possible assistance from heaven and earth? And can we have the heart to refuse them any encouragement in our power, especially in their preparations for this glorious work? No; my honored

FOREWORD

friends and gentlemen, let us no longer lie in a state of indifference and disunion; but let us all, to a man, join our hearts, our purses, and our prayers, in this dearest and best of all causes; and, instead of starting frivolous objections, to diminish or cool the generous dispositions of any, let us rather fan the fire into a brighter flame, and love those persons best, who are the most able and ready to promote so good a work!

And now, my dear honored friends, are these things so? Is the design of the Christian ministry the greatest and noblest that God ever decreed to put into the heart of man? Is it the end of the Christian preacher's office to bring millions of immortal souls out of the ruins of the fall, into the riches of eternity; to recover souls from sin to holiness, from rebellion to obedience; from filthiness to purity; from the most horrid deformity, to the perfection of beauty; from guiltiness, to full justification by a divine and infinite righteousness; from misery to happiness; from the curse of God, to eternal blessings; from the deepest disgrace, to the highest honor; from extreme poverty, to unbounded riches; from slavery to the devil, to liberty in Christ; from the spirit and temper of a wicked world, to the spirit and dignity of the sons of God; from the ravages of moral death, to the pleasures of eternal life; from the darkness of hell, to the light of heaven; from violent enmity, to the most intense love of God; from the attachment of the passions to lust, to the full flow of affections to Christ, as the supreme Beauty and Good; from bearing the image of the great apostate spirit, to resemble God in a brighter manner than the angels in heaven?

Are these the sublime ends of the Christian ministry; and is this to be the continual and noble work of every true Christian preacher?

Directions for a Candidate of the Ministry

Then, my dear friends, what encouragement should you give towards the regular education of pious and sensible young men for this noble and divine office!

Permit me, my honored friends, to proceed a little farther, to awaken your attention, and to rouse your generous zeal to encourage all serious and sensible young men who appear firm to be ministers of the gospel. Let me propose the following queries to your serious consideration.

Is not a wise Christian minister the greatest character under heaven? If we compare him with all other characters in life, will not his shine brighter on the comparison, as much as the sun in the expanse of heaven out-shines a poor glow-worm in a ditch? If you compare him with a physician in a hospital, a counselor in his chambers, an advocate at the bar, a merchant in his commerce, a judge on his seat, an ambassador in the court of kings, a banker amidst his treasures, a general at the head of an army, a representative of his country, a lord in parliament, or a monarch on his throne—yea, to go higher still, compare him with the stars of heaven, or an angel in glory; and a gospel minister will shine brighter on the comparison, and appear far above all the offices and characters in the whole world.

The greatest men that ever lived were preachers of the gospel; witness Enoch, the seventh from Adam; witness Noah, Moses, David, Solomon, Isaiah, and Paul; and let me dare so far to magnify the office, as to affirm, that if Kings did but know and feel the dignity, importance, usefulness, and ends of the Christian ministry; they would *descend* from their thrones, to *ascend* the pulpit, as a throne of much greater glory.

What preparation, then, does this office deserve and demand; and how serious, how attentive, how active, and unweariedly diligent ought every student to be who desires and designs to employ himself in this glorious work to the end of his life! With what ardor and gratitude should he seize every help and guide to his highest end! With what eagerness and delight should he embrace every means, and every friend, who is wise enough, and able to help him forwards in the grand design of preaching the glorious gospel!

My dear young friends, let me now address you. Do not your hearts burn with celestial fire, to be employed in the noblest work under heaven? yea, let me not be extravagant, if I affirm that it is such a manner of serving and glorifying God, as cannot be practiced, even in heaven itself. It is such a work as, in some respects exceeds the work of heaven.[1] There are no sinners to be converted there; no devils to be resisted; no conflicts with internal corruption; no living by faith on an invisible God and Savior; no scorn to encounter; no persecutions and cruel mocking to be borne; but here we have them all; so that we have such graces to be exercised, and such difficulties to be encountered, as will never be found in heaven to eternity.

Amongst all the various books[2] which have been written for the use of students of divinity and Christian preachers, I

---

[1] As preachers perform work which angels cannot do, so they are nearer to God's throne, and dearer to Christ than even angels, even now, in this life; Revelation 4:6, The angels surround the living creatures, chap. 5:2.

[2] The principal books written for the use of Students and Preachers that I am acquainted with, are the following: (1) John Chrysostom, *On the Priesthood*; (2). John Wilkins, *Preacher*. There are judicious thoughts, and the best collection of books that were then extant, in this excellent treatise; John Edwards, *The Preacher*; Richard Baxter, *The Reformed Pastor*; Isaac Watts, *Humble Attempt*, which exceeds all the former; François Fénelon, *Dialogues on the Eloquence of the Pulpit*; Blaise Gisbert, *Christian Eloquence in Theory and Practice*; David Fordyce, *Theodorus*, or a *Dialogue on Preaching*; Jean Claude,

know of none equal to the *Manuductio* of Dr. Cotton Mather, especially if you consider the smallness of the treatise, and the peculiar pertinency and pungency of the thoughts contained in it.

I have been intimately acquainted with this excellent little book for thirty-six years past; I first met with it in the study of my dear and honored friend and father, the Rev. Mr. Hugh Evans of Bristol, when I boarded at his house in the years 1744, 1745, 1746. The book has been of exceeding great use to me ever since. I am sorry I did not publish it sooner for the benefit of the rising generation of gospel ministers. It is with great satisfaction and delight that I have done it now. Sensible, inquisitive, and pious young students lie very near my heart. I feel a strong parental affection for them. I earnestly pray that they may rise to superior eminence in every part of their glorious employment. I shall rejoice to see them actuated with the noble and divine ambition to excel their predecessors, in wisdom, dignity, zeal, and diligence; and to see them glorify Christ, and allure a vast number of immortal souls into a vital union with the supreme truth, goodness, and beauty, and thus be forever happy in his glorious presence, and infinite love.

To my own dear son, I do peculiarly present this treatise, with my additional notes and observations; and through his

---

An Essay on the Composition of a Sermon. This is the largest work, and full of rich notes; Richard Blackmore, *The Accomplished Preacher*. This book is little known, in proportion to its worth and excellence; Thomas Gibbons, *The Christian Minister*. Here you have a thousand good hints respecting the reading of the best authors, the composing of sermons, and the prudent conduct of life; James Fordyce, *The Eloquence of the Pulpit*; James Fordyce, *An Essay on Pronunciation*; John Mason, *On Pronunciation*; *On Public Speaking*, translated from the French; John Ryland, *Christian Preacher Delineated*.

Foreword

hands, I devote it to the service of modest, pious students of all denominations. I leave it as a monument and proof of my tenderest affection to the churches of Christ, who are deeply interested in its contents; and shall rejoice to find that wise and religious gentlemen of property are stirred up to do their very utmost towards encouraging a learned and evangelical education of worthy young men, who shall be ministers of the glorious gospel when our heads are laid in the dust, and our souls adoring the Son of God in the realms of light and glory.

John Ryland
Northampton,
October 7, 1781.

Directions for a
Candidate of the Ministry

1
Death Realized

Intending to give you some directions for your proceeding in the studies upon which you are entering, that you may be prepared and furnished for the work of the Evangelical ministry, to which you are designed; I shall not consult the method which any of the twice twelve, *Dissertationes de Studiis* (collected by Elzivir in one little volume), have given you. But the contemplation of death shall be the first point of the wisdom that my advice must lead you to.

In the first place, my son, I advise you to consider yourself as a dying person, and one that must shortly put off this earthly tabernacle. I move you, I press you, to remember how short your time is, yea, though it should reach to the longest that is ordinarily known among the children of men; and how much shorter it may be made for ought you know in the early anticipations of mortality. Do this, that you may do nothing like living in vain. Place yourself in the circumstances of a dying person—your breath failing, your throat rattling, your eyes with a dim cloud, and your hands with a damp sweat upon them, and your weeping friends no longer able to retain you with them. And then entertain such sentiments of this world, and of the work to be done in this world, that such a view must needs inspire you withal.

Such a numbering of your days, I hope, will compel you to apply your heart unto wisdom; and instruct and excite you to spend your little time in such things, and so industriously, as may be a matter of comfortable reflection at the end of your days. The apprehension of a dying person are usually so wise, and so much have the right thoughts of the righteous in them, that the best counsel which can be given you is, "Child, make haste unto them!" It cannot be too soon to come into them. They will have a mighty tendency to make you serious, discreet, and industrious, and every way well advised; and all that your best friends would have you to be.

You run the hazard of dying without wisdom, if you delay to come into them; and put far away that which by doing so you will make an evil day. It was not a folly in some of the Ancients to assign *the contemplation of death* as the main foundation and main exercise of their philosophy. And the young man will arrive to more understanding than the Ancients who does practice upon it. I propose a *Vive memor Mortis,*[1] as what will be the way to the truest wisdom, and no little part of it; and as what will contribute as much as possible for anything to do, unto a wise conduct in all your affairs.

May the *thoughts of a dying man* come into an early and lively consideration with you, and regulate your intentions, your appetites, your behaviors. My proposal is that you would set apart proper times (and be sure, the present time!) to think: What sort of life shall I most approve when I come to die?! In what work shall I most wish to have lived when I see that I am to die? What method and manner of living shall I apprehend the most eligible when my dying hour is come upon me?

---

[1] Translation: "Live mindful of death."

Death Realized

Behold, what will give to the young man knowledge and discretion?!

2
THE TRUE END OF LIFE

The apprehension of approaching death, one would think, should make you as soon as may be begin to live. But you do not begin to live, no, you are dead while you live until you live unto God. Methinks, I have already prepared you to consider the words which before I go any further, I shall transcribe for you from a treatise entitled, *The Angel of Bethesda*, which is yet (I may say, lying at the pool) unpublished:

> Christian, fill your life with most explicit acknowledgements of the Glorious God, and acts of obedience to Him. Let even the whole business of your temporal calling be explicitly designed for an obedience to God. At the same time, fill your life with good offices to mankind, and with actions that shall be blessings (and make the doer a rich one) unto your neighbors. This will be living—*Caetera mortis erunt.*[1] The man who does the most of these things is the longest liver. In three sevens of years, one who lives at this rate may have a longer life than a drowsy and thoughtless wretch that should get along to nine hundred and sixty-nine. I may make the more free with the number in my expression on this occasion,

---

[1] Translation: "The rest belongs to death." Attributed to Vergil, but most likely medieval in origin.

because the Jewish Rabbi's venture to tell us that the time lost by Methuselah in impertinent things being deducted from his nine hundred and sixty-nine years, he will have no more than ten years of true life left unto him. It is a maxim of truth, *Non annis sed factis vivunt mortales.*[2] And, they have lived longest in the world, who have done the most good in the world. So my Angel.

And now, my son, though I began with recommending to you the thoughts of a death at hand; yet, what I mean is, to make a long liver, and in order to it, a true liver, of you.

The true end of life must therefore, as soon as may be, come to be stated and fixed with you, and the false ways of sin be no longer walked in. And what can this end be but the service of the Glorious God? Or, as you have been taught from your infancy, "to glorify God and enjoy Him forever." When you have considered the matter with the deepest meditation, you can settle nowhere but here, and you can see nothing worthy to be the end of living but this? May my life be such a continual homage to the Glorious GOD, as He may through His Christ look down with delight upon. If you terminate in any inferior end and rise no higher in your aims than to have yourself accommodated with such things as a carnal mind calls, comfortable circumstances, your life, what is it but a perpetual folly, on which you may cry out, *O me nunquam sapientem!*[3] All your achievements, though they should be never so pompous, are but empty futilities. Nay, how little higher do you aim than the beasts that perish? And how much will you deserve the

---

[2] Translation: "Mortals live not for length of days but for deeds."

[3] Translation: "I shall never be wise!"

name of brutish, which is the denomination with which your herd is branded in the oracles of God? A little more hair, and crawling upon all four. And, what the difference! But, O star fallen and choked in the dust, arise and shine, and let your light come, and the glory of the Lord be risen upon you! It is brought about, and the true light shines, when you come to make choice of this as the main scope of your living in the world; it shall be that the Glorious God may be gratified, in beholding through His Christ the homage which I pay unto Him; rendering and procuring acknowledgements to Him in all my ways! And wisely subordinate all your actions, and all your enjoyments unto it: Govern your actions by it, and consider them, as parts of that homage; relish your enjoyments from it, and consider them as helps for that homage; and often have your explicit thoughts upon it. Come into those right thoughts of the righteous, with which the ancients were illuminated, when they determined that, *Uti Deo et frui creaturis,*[4] does in short and at once express all the disorder and confusion that mankind is thrown into. Having such a single eye, your whole conduct will be full of light. But if you have none but some inferior end in your eye, you will have an evil eye. Your very light will be darkness; and how great your darkness! From that hour that you come into this life of God, and thus dwell in God, it is inexpressible how comfortably you will walk with God, and have the blessed God ever dwelling in you. The God who forms the spirit of man within him has imprinted on your spirit a tendency of return unto Him. This impression is wretchedly suppressed and sinned away in your fall from God, and the tendency woefully diverted and enfeebled. The faculty, which we

---

[4] Translation: "Use God and delight in his creation."

call the *conscience*, is the testimony of this impression, and is "the work of the Law written in the heart" (Rom. 2:15). If it must continue under its depravations and encumbrances, what remains of it will be only to inflict the eternal scourges, and scorches of a self-condemning mind upon you. Such a recovery of it, as will restore the Most High unto His throne in your soul, so that nothing shall be above Him there, nor shall there be any denial of the God that is above, but the intention of a grateful homage unto the Glorious God shall command your whole conduct; this is the highest felicity that you can aspire unto. The very top of what our great Redeemer has proposed for us is a union with God!

Many things there are that pass for wisdom among the children of this world. But this is the grant point, whereof it may be asserted. Here is wisdom: let him that has understanding pass a judgment upon it. The surname of old put upon our Gildas, belongs unto the children of this wisdom, and unto none but those. Until this point be gained, nothing that is truly wise is to expected from you. But let your accomplishments be what they will, you stand in the list of those that must have it said of them, "What wisdom is there in them?" Nay, since the object which a man makes his last end, the same he makes his God, so many low and base and wrong ends, as those wherein you terminate, until you thus live unto God, are your gods; your life is a course of detestable and abominable idolatries; your portion will be among the idolaters who shall not inherit the Kingdom of God.

It is with the utmost importunity that I press to have this matter well settled with you. Yea, entreat me not to leave you, nor to return from following after you, until you are brought into this way of living, which distinguishes the excellent of the earth from those who are but so many carcasses falling in the wilderness.

That you may not fall into the hypocrisy of many books, which wear the motto of, *Soli Deo Gloria*,[5] upon them, while the author in reality never aimed any higher than his own admired self, but as a truly learned writer detects him, *Scripsitat sibi ipsi, ac famae suae, interdum et fami.*[6] Let me labor a little more to explain this most rational mystery of Godliness.

God is glorified when His infinite perfections are beheld and confessed with a suitable veneration, and His Glorious Christ is considered with the regards which God has required for Him.

The service of God lies in this veneration; and in the doing and using of those things that shall be subservient unto it.

Hence, whatever contributes unto the welfare of mankind, and such a relief of their miseries, as may give the children of men better opportunities to glorify Him, this also is to glorify Him.

In glorifying of God, there must be a *legitima scoporum subordinatio*;[7] and you are perpetually to discern, and to design, the subordination.

But see what provision I shall make for you. I purpose anon to lead you into an acquaintance with various tongues and arts; but I can do nothing until you are acquainted first of all, with what I may call, much more justly than that which has been commonly called *the universal discipline*.

---

[5] Translation: "For the glory of God alone."

[6] Translation: "He writes always for himself, for his fame, and even for his greed."

[7] Translation: "a legitimate subordination of goals."

Wherefore, I will here lay before you a plan of real and regular living, exhibited in an instrument in which one whose purpose and manner of life has been known unto you, stated his method of living unto God. It will be no vanity to say that if the instrument could be shown in as many languages, as Grotius's *de Veritate* has appeared in, or as many as paid their obsequies unto *Peireskius*, yea, or as many as they say are spoken in the city of Cairo, it could meet with no considerate reader, that would not find something within him, that would compel him to justify it.

Here you have, what may challenge the title of, *Imrei Binah*[8] with you.

Sic Vivitur.

With a single eye, to keep up a regular and perpetual aim at the right end of all that I do, and of all that I have; this will be to walk in the light continually. The glory of God is the only right end of all; and it will gloriously lighten the mind that has an eye upon it. But the Lamb is to be at the same time, the light of such a soul, and a Christ is to be considered: God in that Lord of glory is to be the object which my eye must be forever to, if I would not have my foot in the net of the evil ones.

That I may truly live, Oh! may the life of God, and of His Christ be thus manifested in me!

Everything which the candle of the Lord condemns as an evil thing, I would forever abhor it, and avoid it; Because it will incur that rebuke, *By sin thou dishonorest God.*

---

[8] Translation: "Expressions of Wisdom."

I apprehend every act of obedience to God as a thing which the eye of that Infinite One does with pleasure take notice of.

That which procures any act of my obedience to be pleasing unto the Infinite God, is the mediation of my Savoir. He has by His obedience to God for me, made expiation for the defects of my obedience, and bespoke a gracious acceptance for it. This obedience of His, I look upon, and lean upon, as the only righteousness that justifies me. But mine has in it a faint resemblance of that perfect obedience which my Jesus has yielded unto God for me; and it is an obedience, which the Spirit of my Jesus, influencing and actuating of me, is the worker of. Yea, 'Tis more immediately to a glorious Christ, and God shining upon me in Him, that I may pay my obedience.

If I may in any act of obedience or of submission to the will of God, be a grateful spectacle to Him or, if He may take satisfaction in what He helps me to be and to do before Him, this is the highest felicity I can wish for; the top of my ambition; the last end, the main and chief scope of my life. Lord, beyond this, there is nothing that I can ask or think.

Prepared with such sentiments, I proceed now thus to fix my eye upon the right end of all that my hand finds to do, or that God puts into it.

Why do I attend on the daily sacrifices of the closet and of the household?
Lord, I desire now to pay that homage to Thee, which Thou wilt, for the sake of Thy Christ, look down with delight upon.
Why do I give attendance on the public exercises of religion?
Lord, I desire to join with Thy people in paying to Thee those acknowledgements, which Thou art well-pleased withal.

I would also improve in knowledge and in goodness, and so in being what God would have me to be, by conversing with such truths as I now meet withal.

Why do I set myself to read these sacred Scriptures?

Lord, I desire to pay a due regard unto the treasures with which Thou graciously entertainest me. Yea, I would hear, what God the Lord will speak unto me; and be taught what I may speak, and how live unto Him.

Why do I, in the way of my studies, go to fill the chambers of my soul with all precious and pleasant riches?

Lord, I desire to furnish myself with such things, as may render me more qualified for what service Thou mayst call me to.

Why do I compose the discourses, which I exhibit, either in the press or in the pulpit?

Lord, I desire to communicate unto others what may animate them, or accomplish them, for living unto God.

Why do I make any of my visits to any of my neighbors? Or, countenance their visits unto me?

Lord, I desire to let fall something in the conference that may be for the good of the company; even that more may be known of Thee, and done for Thee from what passes in it.

And, when I propose to ingratiate myself unto any people, by the civilities of conversation, it shall be that I may gain thereby the better advantages to prosecute good purposes upon them.

In conversation, I would especially lay hold on all advantages to introduce as much as I can of a lovely Christ into the view of all that I come near unto.

My journeys must like my visits be for nothing, but that God may be served in them.

Why do I eat or drink?

Lord, I desire nothing but that I may be strengthened for the work, which Thou hast assigned unto me.

What of the table, may for quality or quantity, indispose me for Thy work, I will for that cause avoid it.

And I will affect most what I find most useful to me for the work before me. Lord, I would have my appetites entirely regulated from this consideration.

Why do I allow sleep to my eyes or slumber to my eyelids?

Lord, I desire to have my spirits recruited for that work, wherein I delight to do Thy will, O my God.

In using of remedies for the relief of any maladies, I am to be acted from the same consideration; that what hinders me from comfortably proceeding in the work of God, may be removed.

Why do I trim, cleanse, adorn my body?

Lord, I desire to recommend myself unto them, unto whom I would be acceptable in my endeavors to convey something of Thee unto them.

Why do I suffer myself to be persuaded into any brief diversions?

Lord, I desire, that by a little unbending of my bow, and remitting the intenseness of my *Essays to Do Good*, I may the more harden it into a bow of steel; and return with more vigor to the work of my God.

But, I will watch for all opportunities to carry on *Essays to Do Good* in the midst of my diversions.

Why do I write any letters?

Lord, I desire now to do something that that Thou wouldst have to be done. Here is a business that God calls me to.

And, if I can interweave any mention of any matters in and for which, I may bespeak Thee to be adored, it shall be mentioned.

I will add this article to this point of my living unto God. The several petitions which I carry to the Glorious God in my supplications, I would very distinctly examine, What aspect they have upon the service of God? If I can see none, I will drop them and lay them aside. But the view of a holy aspect in them, and if the voice of my supplications truly be, Let God be glorified, that shall invigorate them.

But, finally; what is it that gives me a relish for the comfortable things that are bestowed upon me? What are the things which delight my soul in the comforts which abate the sorrows of my pilgrimage?

Lord, Thou shalt be the joy of my joy.

None of these things are to be my enjoyments; they are to be but instruments.

There are sensual delights, which I may lawfully taste, but always thankfully, in compliance with the order, wherein the God of nature has made them agreeable to the senses. His bounty is to be tasted in them; and as being the effects of that, they are to be delectable.

The sweet of my bodily nourishments must lie, not in their being so much suited unto my palate, as in the support they bring me for the service of my God.

This also is that which makes the rest of the laboring man sweet unto him.

How far are my possessions of lands, or goods, or money, to be sweet unto me? No farther than as they are helps to me, in the work of God. And they are never to be used by me, but when something that I may count a work of God, is to be carried on. All my expenses are to be, on something that God would have to be done: and so to spend, should be as pleasant unto me, as it can be, to gain or save.

When I am a married man, I am doing my duty to God, in conforming to the ninth of Ecclesiastes and the ninth.

My children are valuable, and very relishable things. My Reason is; they are the subjects of Thy kingdom, O my God and Savior: and Thou hast made me related unto them, and they are by Thee committed unto me, as precious things, in singular circumstances, to be through my cultivation and erudition and instruction, more than any others, rendered such servants unto Thee, as Thou mayest account for a Generation.

My friends are some of my good things. That which makes them so, is the good I may do to them, or I may do by them. And further, I would not know them.

Lord, the things which discover Thee to me, shall therefore and so far, be sweet; and the more discovery they make of Thee, the sweeter they shall be, unto me.

What and where my relish for books, which I may be hungry for? Lord, because I shall see Thee, or serve Thee, the more for the reading of them.

I do not merely once for all, settle upon these right end, for the center of my life, and the consecration of my all unto my God and Savior, but I would often, often, even as often as I can, explicitly consider them. And if anything occur, wherein I cannot see these right ends answered, I would be loth to meddle with it.

As an epilogue unto this instrument, I would subject the weighty words, which a dear brother of mine, a professor in the

Directions for a Candidate of the Ministry

Frederician University, who understands this way of living, has upon it:

> *Omnia ita facienda sunt, respectu habito ad Gloriam Dei; ut, etsi non semper actus adsit hujus intentionis, omnia tamen fiant ex* habitu *et* generali proposito *nunquam mutando. Sed tamen* actualis intentio, *et crebra ejus* repetitio, *plurimum prodest. Conscientiam enim conservat tranquillam, animum {que} ob sinceram intentionem bene sibi conscium, reddit Laetum, et in opere ipso alacriorem ac circumspectiorem.*[9]

---

[9] Translation: "Everything must so be done out of respect for the glory of God that, even if the impulse of its intent is not present, nevertheless it all arises from habit and general purpose with never any change. But actual intent, and the frequent repetition of it, yields the most profit. Let him therefore preserve a tranquil conscience, and a mind well conscious of itself through sincere intent (this gives joy!) and quite eager and circumspect in the work itself."

3
Regeneration Essential to a Good Preacher

But you will not come to this until the Glorious God of all grace gives you a new heart and causes a regenerating work of His grace to pass upon you, and by sanctifying impressions of His Holy Spirit upon you, call you to His Glory by Christ Jesus. A carnal mind in you, full of enmity against God, will have a perpetual aversion for this living to Him until He shall, by His verticordious influences, heal the distempers which you have contracted in and by your departure from Him. Your conversion to God must be accomplished, or else you will have no heart, nor skill, nor strength, for that life of piety, which must be laid in the foundation of all the good that is to be expected *by* you, or *from* you.

Now that you may arrive to all the blessedness of a sinner converted from the error of his way and a soul saved from death, I will briefly describe to you that process of repentance which you must go through, and which every man that lives and knows that he shall, but not when he shall see death is out of his wits if he do not immediately come into. For this purpose, I need not alter the direction that my Caelestinus has already given you; you have in unalterable strains had the sum of the matter.

Take a proper season for it, and, my son, the present season; I say, immediately! Therein, first, humbly and indeed, lying in the dust, own yourself unable to do anything effectually of yourself in changing of your heart, and bringing your soul to be informed and affected as it ought to be. Say, "O Glorious God, I justly perish if I do not come unto Thee; but if Thou draw me not, I shall never come unto Thee." Yea, and therewithal, humbly own, that if ever God changes your heart and enable you to do any good thing, there must be triumphs of sovereign grace over the basest and blackest unworthiness in it. Say, "Lord, I am utterly unworthy that Thou, who alone hast the words of eternal life, shouldest ever speak them unto me, and cause me to live."

Under such a humiliation, go on and lay before yourself a catalogue of things forbidden, and things required in the Ten Commandments. Loath and judge yourself before the Lord for the innumerable evils which, beholding yourself in this glass, you will see encompassing of you. Let your contempt of the gospel and your neglect of the Jesus, who would save you from these innumerable evils, be thrown as a yet more heavy weight into the scale. But then, go back as far as your original sin, the sin of the first hearkening to the old serpent, and the venom derived from thence, which is the original of all your actual sins; the corrupt fountain, which has run into the streams of the actual enormities and iniquities with which your life has been polluted. Own upon it: "O great God, Thou art holy and righteous in all the sad things that have ever been inflicted on me, and hast punished me less than my sins deserve. I deserve to be stripped of all that may be at all comfortable to me; I deserve to be scourged with sore plagues and of long continuance; I deserve to be thrown into the place of dragons, and be punished with the devil and his angels."

Now, behold the Son of God made flesh in the blessed Jesus, and proffering to do the part of a Mediator for you; yea, making Himself responsible for the debt of His people to the law of their God. Behold Him undergoing the punishment which was due to you for your sin, and with bloody sufferings making a sufficient expiation that you may not be punished for it. Behold Him fulfilling all righteousness in doing always the things that please the Father; that so you may have a lot among the righteous. Admire the free grace of the Glorious God which allows you to make this plea for your justification. Plead it, that you may be justified. Plead it, with a comfortable persuasion of your finding a kind reception with your Savior. Do not think that you honor, but that you reproach your Savior, if you doubt your kind reception with Him.

At the same time, take up a full purpose of heart that you will cleave unto the Lord. Let your heart be fixed in a strong purpose to deny all ungodliness and worldly lusts, and lead a Godly, and a sober, and a righteous life. But resign yourself up unto your Savior, that He may by His Holy Spirit make you perfect in every good work to do His will, and work in you that which is well pleasing in the sight of God. Wholly despair of doing anything that is holy and just and good, any further than you have your Savior strengthening of you.

Thus you have done what you have to do, that you may lay hold on eternal life. If God be with you in this action, your conversion to God is now accomplished. Everything in heaven and earth and hell now looks with a most joyful aspect upon you.

This, with ardent and constant cries to the gracious God, who gives wisdom to them that ask it of Him, is the way to come into the experience of a principle infused from above into you, that shall be indeed Christ formed in you; and Christ living in you will enable you to do and to bear what you shall in the Christian life be called unto. A principle of piety—even, the love of God—thus produced in you, shall be the root of the righteous; in you, perpetually bringing forth fruits of righteousness, which are by Jesus Christ unto the glory of God. This principle will incline you to endeavor all possible conformity to your Savior in hating and shunning everything that the light of God in you shall condemn as an evil thing; and in filling your life with acts of devotion towards God and benignity towards men; and in behaving yourself as remembering the eye of heaven always upon you; and in approving yourself ever a good steward of the manifold favors that heaven bestows upon you; and in suffering afflictions after a becoming manner; and in hoping and waiting for the joy set before you in the heavenly world. A principle and an attainment and a blessedness, infinitely preferable, not only to all the wealth in the world, but also to all intellectual accomplishments and embellishments: And without which, all the ornaments on which the great men of the earth value themselves are but gilded vanities: Nor will you, being destitute thereof, have any other advantage of the lustres you are seeking after, than to have your lamp go out in obscure darkness, and expire with such a woeful complaint as that; *Qualis artifex pereo!*[1] The meanest laborer with his hands, even a John Urich, having the fear of God in him, will be more excellent than you, or indeed than one who has carried a baton

---

[1] Translation: "As such a great artist I perish," purportedly the last words of Nero.

in his hands, but has gone on without God in the world; and he will come to a better end than that wherein you must mourn at the last, with him who said, *Surgunt indocti et rapiunt caelum; nos cum nostris doctrinis mergimur in infernum.*[2]

I am inexpressibly concerned that you may have an unblemished youth, and not be left unto such falls now in your youth as may cause you to go halting all your days: yea, that you may be such a pure Nazarite, and preserved more particularly from criminal and abasing unchastities, and most particularly from detestable Onanism, that you may be able to say, "Ah, Lord God, my soul has not been polluted from my youth up." I cannot think of a more effectual preservative than such a conversion to God, as I now exhort you to.

---

[2] Translation: "The unlearned rise and seize the sky while we, with our doctrines, sink into hell." This is a paraphrase of Augustine, *Confessions* 8.8.

4
A ZEAL TO DO GOOD

Certainly, you will be brought now without much difficulty to what I next proceed unto! Being thus brought into an happy state of reconciliation to God, you are prepared, yea, you cannot but be disposed now to hearken unto such subordinate counsels as I am now to offer you: whereof the first will be that *Essays to Do Good*[1] may fill your life, and be the very spirit and business of it, and the principal delight. The motto which an English lord has upon his coat of arms is what I propose to your continual ambition; *Ut prosim.*[2] And, my son, my advice to you is, begin betimes to take that noble question into consideration: what good may I be capable of doing in the world? Have stated and proper times for it, and these as often as may be, to consider on the question; and keep a record of your purposes.

First, with a humble and mournful sense of your own barrenness, and sensible how much you want that wisdom, which is to find out well-advised inventions, look up to God your Savior, that by Him (who is the wisdom of God) living in you, and leading of you, you may obtain a fair view of the opportunities

---

[1] Also known as *Bonifacius* (1710). One of Mather's most famous works on the fruit of sanctification.

[2] Translation: "That I may be of use." The motto of Virginia Tech, which they render as "That I may serve."

Directions for a Candidate of the Ministry

to do good, which He has put into your hand, that they may not be a price in the hand of a fool; and a clear view of the methods to be taken that this good may be prosecuted and your desire sweetly accomplished. Then proceed and enquire.

Enquire, first: what shall I do for myself, that I may myself improve in knowledge and goodness; and the ends of those means, which the divine cultivation employs upon me?

Enquire, next: what shall I do for my several relatives, my kindred according to the flesh; that I may prove a blessing in each of my relations? Take a catalogue of them; and successively bestow distinct thoughts upon them all.

Then go on to take some cognizance of the several societies to which you stand related, especially the church whereof you are a member (and the college, if you belong to that!); yea, the town, and the land, whereof you are an inhabitant.

Think: What good is to be proposed and promoted here! To what an extent, O dear son, and pleasant child, may your projections carry you!

Particular persons in your neighborhood may now also be found out as objects that good may be done unto; the poor for to be relieved; the sick for to be visited; the sad for to be comforted; and those that are out of the way, to be reclaimed from the error of their way. Many of those whom you have distinguished in thus doing of good unto them, you will find prove monsters of ingratitude. But let not this dishearten you. God is now trying of you, whether you will do good for the pure sake of good; and you will this way have recompenses ascertained unto you in the harvest when, whatsoever good thing any man does, the same shall he receive of the Lord.

But, because your own capacities to do good may be greatly limited, you should also have a time to think; what good lying out of my reach may I see others capable of doing more than I? And hereupon become a humble adviser unto them. Yea, I could wish you would betimes make it a rule for your conduct that you will, as far as you can, always endeavor a profitable conversation; and in every company, think whether you may not with decency let fall some word, which they may be the wiser or the better for; and every one go from you, *Aut doctior, aut melior*,³ for you.

Your opportunities to do good may at first be very small and under very narrow limitations. Nevertheless, I press you to begin betimes, your enquiries after them, and your actions upon them; and expect that though the beginning be but small the latter end shall greatly increase. That word, *Habenti dabitur*,⁴ will be remarkably and conspicuously fulfilled unto you, by the all-governing providence of him who has all opportunities to do good entirely at his disposal. Your circles will grow wider and wider, and anon expand unto dimensions beyond what you could at first have imagined. And, I hope, you will esteem your opportunities as your incomparable treasures. While others are hunting and grasping after the sordid wealth of this world, which will presently be found all "vanity, vanity!"—You will reckon your advantages to promote the kingdom of God, and the welfare of men, as much more valuable riches. You will be as thankful to anyone who informs you of a point wherein you may do some good, as if he had presented you with a wedge of gold: and your maxim will be, *Divitiis abundet per me licet, quisquis voluerit; In operibus mea sit abundantia.*⁵

---

³ Translation: "Either more learned, or better."
⁴ Translation: "To one who has, it will be given."
⁵ Translation: "May he abound in riches through me, whoever wishes. In my works let there be abundance."

DIRECTIONS FOR A CANDIDATE OF THE MINISTRY

But then, you must not be so weak as to imagine that this way of living will recommend you to the favor of this world. A sedulous doer of good will certainly find himself more exposed than other men to be ill-spoken of; greatly maligned, reviled, slandered. Here, patience must have its perfect work. I may say, here is the patience of the saints. Yea, I must say, be very courageous.

I will conclude this matter with the words of one who knew what he wrote:

> Were a man able to write in seven languages: could he converse daily with the sweets of all the liberal sciences, that polite men ordinarily pretend unto; did he entertain himself with all the ancient and modern histories; and could he feast continually on the curiosities, which all sorts of learning may bring unto him: none of all this will afford the ravishing satisfaction, much less would any grosser delights of the senses do it, which he might find in relieving the distresses of a poor, mean, miserable neighbor; and which he might much more find in doing any extensive service for the kingdom of our great Savior in the world, or anything to redress the miseries under which mankind is generally languishing.

5
THE RIGHT END OF STUDIES

You are now in the pursuit of that learning, and those ingenuous and mollifying arts which may distinguish you from the more uncultivated part of mankind, and may accomplish you to claim a place among them who are the blessings and beauties of their generation. Concerning this, what I do in the first place advise you to is, to fix the end of all your studies, and let this be what it ought to be. Let Vives's Motto, *Oculus ad scopum*,[1] have its influence upon you in your whole course of all your studies. If you aim no higher nor better than to render yourself considerable, and make a figure among your fellow-mortals, or, perhaps, to gain a comfortable subsistence in the world, all you do is wrong and mean, and vile, and the Holy God looks down with abhorrence upon you. A Bernard is not the only Christian who has had a true sight of the vanity with which the studies of the most that seek after knowledge are carried on, and pronounced those the only right students, *Qui ad hoc volunt intelligere ut benefaciant.*[2] I hope it would not be unintelligible unto you if I should recommend unto your emulation a flight of one who, though I find him in the cursed city, herein spoke like one of

---

[1] Translation: "Eyes on the goal."
[2] Translation: "Those who wish for this reason to learn, that they do well."

ours: "Lord, I had rather, could it be without sin, that all should hate me than that they should love me for myself: if all the world hate me, I should have but what is mine; if they should love me for myself, they would usurp what is Thine."

But thus much I cannot but wish for, that you may betimes be inspired with sentiments by which the idol that has more votaries than that on the plain of Dura, that is to say, *self* may be dethroned with you. Be aware of it, that the most of people who shall honor you, and admire you, and applaud you, will terminate in you, and look no further than the worm they look next upon: God will not have His praises in what is done for you and by you. God, without whom and before whom, you are as nothing, will not be remembered; and all will be as nothing, in remembrances of none but ashes. A sacrilegious idolatry will be committed!

But a true servant of God will even deprecate it, as an infelicity, to be made the object of this idolatry: and wish, "Lord, let those that fear Thee (and will see Thee through me), be those that shall turn unto me." The love of God must make you choose rather to be left unregarded in the world than to have those regards paid unto you, wherein the infinite God, the first and the last, shall be robbed of His glory, which He will not give unto another. Yea, be prepared for obscurities, and for indignities, and be reconciled unto them upon this account, I am now delivered from any danger that the robbers of God may make an idol of me! But having thus forbidden you the wrong ones, I will tell you, what is the right end unto which it were to be wished, that your studies may be consecrated.

When you are upon seeking an acquaintance with any languages, let your aims be these: "I desire to come at those treasures, which these tongues may be keys unto; and this, that so I

Right End of Studies

may be the better furnished for that service of God, which I may be called unto."

When you are upon seeking an acquaintance with any sciences, let your aims be these: "I desire to gain those illuminations which may be necessary for an instrument of good unto others." And this: "That so I may be the better qualified for that service of God, which will require a workman that need not be ashamed."

When you are upon reading any book, let your aims forever be of the same importance.

To strengthen my advice, I will transcribe some words of the celebrated Lord Chief Justice Hale, who in his account of the good steward, says,

> I carried along with me, in all my studies, this great design of improving them, and the knowledge acquired by them, to the Honor of God's name, and the greater discovery of His wisdom and power and truth, and so translated my secular learning into an improvement of divine knowledge. And had I not practiced this design in my acquists of humane learning, I had concluded my time misspent; because I ever thought it unworthy of a man that had an everlasting soul, to furnish it only with such learning, as would either die with his body, and so become unuseful for his everlasting state, or that in the next moment after death would be attained without labor or toll in this life.

Having thus fixed the right end of your studies, let the view of it make such an impression upon you as to produce a marvelous industry in your prosecution of it. And quicken you to observe that maxim, "Do with thy might, what thy hand finds to do." Remember this, there never was an Eminent who was not an industrious man. You must be diligent in your business, if you would hope to stand in any desirable circumstances before that great King, unto whose holy service you are dedicated.

That you may not suffer a vile impediment in your studies, and avocation from them, I do now particularly warn you against the senseless folly of an entanglement in any foolish amour while you are yet a student at the college. 'Tis time enough to think of marriage when your condition in other circumstances, as well as that of age, will qualify you to make a wise choice, in a point, which a very great felicity, or a very great calamity, for the rest of your days, will turn upon.

6
Study of the Languages

The regulation of your studies is what I would now proceed unto. And for this, though the *Regulae studiorum*, written by Chytraeus, be a book which I can heartily commend unto your perusal, yet it being written an hundred and twenty years ago, I shall not think the perusal of that sufficient for a student in our days. I must further accommodate you.

Latin
And here, humanity would complain of me if I should forbear to tell you that the Latin tongue, which is more known and used than any upon earth except the Arabic, is what you should for many reasons labor to be ready at; and able not only to write, but also to speak in it, with fluency as well as purity; and confute the common observation that though Englishmen do often write (call Spencer and Burnet for two witnesses) the best Latin in the world, yet they often speak it but indifferently. For this purpose you will do well frequently, both to employ your pen, for composing discourses or epistles in it; and likewise to maintain frequent conferences in it, with such as understand the phrases and beauties of it. Indeed, I know not a prettier way than this; translate into English the paragraphs of some author who writes very good Latin (say, the *Enchiridion Precum* of a

Boehm); and then again, laying aside your author, turn your own English into Latin; and so compare that with, and correct it from your authors.

But at the same time, you should familiarize yourself with the style of some authors whose Latin cannot but ever charm you with its elegancies. On this occasion, I am as far from inviting you into the gust of Linacre, as great a critic as most we have had for the Latin tongue, who, *Ciceronis dictionem, nunquam probare potuit, nec sine fastidio audire;*[1] As I am, from inviting you into the Ciceronian bigotry of a Bembo, or, to be as afraid as Longolius was of using the word, *Possibile*. But yet I will presume upon so much of paradox as to offer you my opinion (though I know what censure a Quintilian would pass upon me for saying), that the Latin of an Erasmus, of a Calvin, or of a Witsius, is preferable unto Cicero's; yea, to make up the mess, I am content that poor Castellio, too, be introduced.

Greek

From Rome you must needs pass to Greece. And I cannot but wish you so much a Grecian, as not only to understand your Greek [New] Testament better than they do ordinarily at this day in Athens, in which, of all places, it seems they now speak the worst Greek that is anywhere spoken; but also, that you may at least be able to read a Chrysostom of the Savilian edition; and not enjoy the Fathers only in the Latin translations, in which alone, the Roman Catholics (agreeably indeed unto the name of their church) now generally choose to publish them and peruse them.

---

[1] Translation: "Was never able to approve the diction of Cicero, nor to hear it without loathing."

However, I can't encourage you to throw away much time upon an accurate skill in the Greek accents, but rather wholly to drop them when your quill comes to convey any Greek into your pages. For, as the writing of Greek otherwise than in capitals was introduced in later ages by the monks of Egypt who borrowed the smaller letters now used from the Coptic, so one shall hardly find any accents on the Greek in any manuscripts written above eight ages ago. Nor was the invention of the accents with which our Greek is now encumbered of any other than a musical intention. And Vossius, with Henninius after him, are not the only gentlemen who have declared earnestly against pronouncing the Greek according to the accents: I pray, how would a verse of Homer sound if it were so pronounced?

Hebrew

But for the Hebrew, I am importunate with you. And the more so, because 'tis one remarkable instance of the depraved gust into which we are of later years degenerated, that the knowledge of the Hebrew is fallen under so much disrepute as to make a learned man almost afraid of owning that he has anything of it, lest it should bring him under the suspicion of being an odd, starved, lank sort of a thing, who had lived only on Hebrew roots all his days. What would an Amama, and the rest of the brave men, who shone in the former age, and had souls like the gates of a temple, say, if they might rise and see the men of this generation!

'Tis true, the knowledge of the Hebrew is, contrary to the old maxim, *Difficilia quae pulchra*,[2] with very little difficulty attained unto. Even our little damsels like Blaesilla, the daughter

---

[2] Translation: "What is difficult is excellent."

of Paula (concerning the mother of whom Jerome reports the same that he does of the daughter) make nothing of coming at this uncommon ornament. And Cooper says, truly, that if students would spend as much time at it in a morning or an evening as they misspend on an unprofitable pipe of tobacco, they would in a few days be masters of it. It is also to be owned, that there appears nothing more impertinent than a little Hebrician vaporing and swaggering, as if he had all the learning in the world; and laying hold on all occasions to throw out a Hebrew clause or word for nothing but the ostentation of his mighty accomplishment.

Nevertheless, the knowledge of the Hebrew is to be valued and pursued on this design: it will enable you to penetrate further into the deep things which the Spirit of God has laid up in His oracles than you could possibly do by seeing them only in some translation. Though with much more cause than the modest Melanchthon, I may confess *Me vix primis labiis degustasse Hebraicas literas*,[3] yet as he declared, what Hebrew he had helped him so much in his judgment of the greatest matters, he preferred it before all the wealth of a kingdom. So, I may humbly declare, I scarce ever take a Hebrew Bible into my hands, but I am gratefully surprised with something I never thought of; I ever have some new view, and see something I never saw before. So that I do not wonder at Luther for making a serious protestation, that what knowledge he had of the Hebrew was of more use and more price to him than the greatest heap of gold that could be set before him.

---

[3] Translation: "I hardly ever have touched upon Hebrew letters."

Syriac

Indeed, I cannot but wish that a knowledge of the Syriac may come in as an appendix to your knowledge of the Hebrew, not merely because it was the mother-tongue unto the writers of the New Testament (which is the reason that we have no Greek word of the dual number in all the New Testament; for that number is what the Syriac is a stranger to), but chiefly because the most valuable and serviceable version that we have of the divine oracles, and what may be of most authority in many important points to clear up the sense of them, is the Syriac. And having once got the Hebrew, you'll find the Syriac easily come-at-able.

Modern languages

For the living tongues, 'tis a matter of some speculation that almost all the Protestants in the world, speak the Teutonic and what is derived from it; almost all the Romanists are found in the derivations from the Latin; the Greek Church is mostly in the Sclavonic. If you intend any service to the kingdom of God abroad, you may here take your choice. But if you have any time in your short life to spare for the living tongues, the French will be sure in the first place to court you. And though the complement which the nations of Europe have paid unto that language has looked like a paving of the way (which doubtless, the French academy have had in their eye), for the extending of a covetous and ambitious monarchy, to what will never be accomplished; yet, for the sake of your admission to the reading of many French books that may be worth your perusal, I do not forbid your learning of it. This, the rather, for that albeit the

English tongue is capable of being made the most expressive, and the most copious in the world, and is in these regards much superior to the French. Nevertheless, it may be observed, there is no man who has the French tongue, but ordinarily he speaks the neater English for it.

And yet, concerning the languages in general, the time allowed for them should certainly be proportioned unto the use you are like to make of them. Dr. More, governing himself in the study of the Oriental tongues by that rule, pleasantly and modestly compared himself unto the man who passed by a garrison with a horse shoe at his girdle; which received and repelled the bullet shot upon him: on which he observed that a little armor, if well placed, will be sufficient. I have known one who has been able to compose and publish things in seven languages, and yet confessed to his friends that he could never get the time to furnish himself with much more than the armor of his well-placed horse shoe. But be sure, so much of the armor as you cannot but foresee you may have occasion for—so much I insist upon. I am far from urging you to study so many languages as the epitaph of that great and good physician Kirstenius, ascribed unto him the knowledge of.

7
STUDY OF THE SCIENCES

The languages you will consider but as instruments to come at the sciences, wherewith you would propose to go skillfully about the work which your God shall call you to. And esteeming them as rather helps to erudition than any parts of it, you will no more value yourself as a scholar for them than the bare having of tools would make one to boast himself an artist.

If you would make a short work of all the sciences, and find out a northwest passage to them, I cannot think of any one author that would answer every intention so well as Alsted. I take him to have been as learned a man as ever was in the world; and there being so little use made of his concise exhibitions is, to me, one of the things that I can't but wonder at, and scarce know what to make of.

On rhetoric
Instead of squandering away your time on the rhetoric, whereof no doubt, you thought, your Dugard gave you enough at school; and upon all the tropes and schemes whereof a just censurer well observes, *Possunt una atque; altera hora ita notari, ut*

corum notitia per omnem aetatem sufficiat;[1] and the very profession whereof usually is little more than to furnish out a stage-player; my advice to you is that you observe the flowers and airs of such writings, as are most in reputation for their elegancy. Yet I am willing that you should attentively read over Smith's *Mystery of Rhetoric Unveiled*, that you may not be ignorant of what figures they pretend unto.

But I will take this opportunity to tell you that there is nowhere to be found any such rhetoric as there is in our Sacred Scriptures. Even a pagan Longinus himself will confess the sublime shining in them. There can be nothing so beautiful or so affectuous as the figures everywhere used in them. They are life. All mere human flourishes are but chaff to the wheat that is there. Yea, they are a hammer that breaks the rocks to pieces. In them the God of glory thunders, yea, does it very marvelously! There is in them that voice of the Lord which is full of majesty. For the pulpit-oratory, which is what you have in view, there can be nothing more advisable than to be a master of Scripture phrases and employ them, with an agreeable ingenuity, on all fit occasions. I will add, I know not but a Lamy, in his *L'Art de Parler*, may give you some hints that may be not un-useful to you.

On logic

Nor can I encourage you to spend very much time in that which goes under the name of logic. If my excellent friend Langius, in his noble *Medicina Mentis* (which I commend unto you, to be diligently perused as an introduction to all your studies of the sciences), had not compelled me to a contempt of the vulgar

---

[1] Translation: "They are able so to be recorded at one time or another that knowledge of the heart suffices through every age."

logic learned in our colleges, as a sort of mere morology, yet a little serious recollection would have brought me to it. What is there usually got by the vulgar logic, but only to be furnished with a parcel of terms, which instead of leading the mind into the truth, enables one rather to carry on altercations and logomachies, by which the force of truth may be at pleasure, and by some little trick, evaded.

The power and process of reason is natural to the soul of man. And those masters of reason, who argue the most rationally, and make the most rational researches into the true state of things, and who take the most reasonable measures for their conduct, and who in all things arrive to the most notable discoveries, I pray, what sort of logicians are they? Either they never once read a page of any Burgesdicius, or else they have unlearned and forgot all their vulgar logic. I am sure, they rarely trouble their heads to recall the old rules which they have recited unto their tutors. To exhibit in the pompous form of an art, what everyone does by mere nature and custom, and fabricate it into such a shape as that of the vulgar logic, and with such trifling applications and illustrations, as 'tis usually done, appears as impertinent, as if one should with much formality teach the art of eating or drinking or walking. And it might with equal solemnity be shown what points of regular management are exemplified by the boys playing at their marbles.

The most valuable thing in logic, and the very termination of it, is *the doctrine of syllogisms.* And yet it is notorious that as all syllogizing is only to confirm you in a truth which you are already the owner of, so no logic has yet given us all the several ways of syllogizing that may be run into; and it is as notorious that while an expanded syllogizing is reckoned no other than an indecency in ordinary writing as well as talking, our only syllogizing is that which we call, an enthymeme: such a thing is evident, and therefore such a thing to be inferred from it, is also evident. Notwithstanding, lest we should offend them, go dip into your logic. But count it enough, if you have gone through a Milton, or a Gutberleth, or a Watts. Indeed, some treatises, that clear up the maxims of reason, and may strengthen you and sharpen you in the use of it, you may do well to look into. The *Ars Cogitandi* may pass for one of those: and though for some reasons, I would be excused from recommending an essay of humane understanding, which is much in vogue, yet I can approve your perusing of Oldfield, his *Improvement of Reason*. But for the vulgar logic, I must freely say, you lose time if you steer any otherwise in it, than, touch and go.

On metaphysics

What I say of logic, I say of metaphysics; which a learned man too justly calls, *Disciplinarum omnium excrementum*,[2] though she would set up for the queen of sciences. If you have got a Maccovius, or a Jacchaeus into your head, you have as much as I should care for: to which indeed some acquaintance with a Castanaeus, or some such fencer for distinctions, may be added. But then to weave any more cobwebs in your brains; to what purpose is it? This, however, is one of the things which I will affirm constantly, that as a Suarez, than whom you cannot easily find a greater dealer in metaphysics, after all declared, the hours which he took in studying and examining and rectifying his own heart were of infinitely more use and worth to him than all his metaphysical and voluminous lucubrations. You shall in like manner find that you may easily employ your

---

[2] Translation: "The excrement of all learning."

hours to better purpose than in metaphysical and imaginary disquisitions.

On ethics
As for ethics, though such things as the *Ethica Christiana* of a Daneus, be among the things which cannot be spoken against, yet of that whereon they employ the plough so long in many academies, I will venture to say, 'tis a vile thing; and no other than what honest Vockerodus has justly called it; *Impietas in artis formam redacta.*[3] It is all over a sham; it presents you with a mock happiness. It prescribes to you mock virtues for the coming at it. And it pretends to give you a religion without a Christ, and a life of piety without a living principle; a good life with no other than dead works filling of it. It is not amiss for you to know what this paganism is, and therefore you may, if you please, bestow a short reading upon a Golius, or a More. But be more of a Christian than to look on the *Enchiridion* of the author last mentioned, as next the Bible, the best book in the world. Study no other ethics but what is in the Bible; and consult such books, as the *Verus Christianismus* of an Arndt, whereby hundreds of thousands have been brought into the life of God.

Rules of behavior
So much ethics as treats, *De decoro*, and may instruct you in the rules of behavior, I heartily commend unto you. And yet, even these are best learned by a wise observation of what you see

---

[3] Translation: "Impiety reduced to the appearance of art."

passes in the conversation of politer people, and by wisely considering how they are indeed all contained in that one word, *modesty*; which renders everyone his due, and assumes nothing undue to oneself: or, comprised in that one maxim, "Do and say nothing that may be justly offensive to the company." The truth is, the most exact and constant rules of behavior will be found rules of Christianity: for which cause it pleased our glorious Redeemer more than once to give them. Every Christian as far as he keeps to his own rules will be so far a gentleman. And for this cause, I again advise you to a careful study of them.

8
Poetry & Style

Poetry, whereof we have now even an Antediluvian piece in our hands, has from the beginning been in such request that I must needs recommend unto you some acquaintance with it. Though some have had a soul so unmusical, that they have decried all verse as being but a mere playing and fiddling upon words; all versifying, as if it were more unnatural than if we should choose dancing instead of walking; and rhyme, as if it were but a sort of morisco dancing with bells: yet I cannot wish you a soul that shall be wholly unpoetical.

An old Horace has left us an art of poetry, which you may do well to bestow a perusal on. And besides your lyric hours, I wish you may so far understand an epic poem, that the beauties of a Homer and a Virgil may be discerned with you. As to the moral part of Homer, it is true, and let me not be counted a Zoilus for saying so, that by first exhibiting their gods as no better than rogues, he set open the floodgates for a prodigious inundation of wickedness to break in upon the nations, and was one of the greatest apostles the devil ever had in the world. Among the rest that felt the ill impressions of this universal corrupter (as men of the best sentiments have called him), one was that overgrown robber of execrable memory, whom we celebrate under the name of Alexander the Great; who by his

DIRECTIONS FOR A CANDIDATE OF THE MINISTRY

continual admiring and studying of his *Iliad*, and by following that false model of heroic virtue set before him in his Achilles, became one of the worst of men, and at length inflated with the ridiculous pride of being himself a deity, exposed himself to all the scorn that could belong unto a lunatic. And hence, notwithstanding the veneration which this idol has had, yet Plato banishes him out of a common-wealth, the welfare whereof he was concerned for. Nevertheless, custom or conscience obliges him to bear testimonies unto many points of morality. And it is especially observable, that he commonly propounds prayer to heaven as a most necessary preface unto all important enterprises; and when the action comes on too suddenly for a more extended supplication, he yet will not let it come on without an ejaculation; and he never speaks of any supplication but he brings in a gracious answer to it.

I have seen a travesteering high-flyer, not much to our dishonor, scoff at Homer for this; as making his actors to be like those whom the English call dissenters. But then, we are so much led into the knowledge of antiquities, by reading of this poet, and into so many parts of the recondite learning, that notwithstanding some little nods in him, not a few acute pens besides the old bishop of Thessalonica's have got a reputation by regaling us with annotations upon him. Yea, though one can't but smile at the fancy of Croese, who tries with much ostentation of erudition, to show that Homer has all along tendered us in a disguise and fable, the history of the Old Testament, yet many illustrations of the sacred Scriptures, I find are to be fetched from him; who indeed had probably read what was extant of them in his days; particularly, our eighteenth Psalm is what he has evidently imitated. Virgil too, who so much lived upon him, as well as after him, is unaccountably mad upon his

OF POETRY & STYLE

fate, which he makes to be he knows not what himself, but superior to gods as well as to men, and through his whole composures he so asserts the doctrine of this nonsensical power, as is plainly inconsistent with all virtue.

And what fatal mischief did fascinator do to the Roman Empire, when by deifying one great emperor, he taught the successors to claim the adoration of gods while they were perpetrating the crimes of devils? I will not be a Carbilius upon him; nor will I say anything, how little the married state owes unto one who writes as if he were a woman hater: nor what his blunders are about his poor-spirited and inconsistent hero, for which many have taxed him. Nevertheless, it is observed, that the Pagans had no rules of manners that were more laudable and regular than what are to be found in him. And some have said, "It is hardly possible seriously to read his works without being more disposed unto goodness, as well as being agreeably entertained." Be sure, had Virgil written before Plato, his works had not been any of the books prohibited. But then, this poet also has abundance of rare antiquities for us.

And such things, as others besides a Servius, have imagined that they have instructed and obliged mankind by employing all their days upon. Wherefore if his *Aeneid*, which though it were once near twenty times as big as he has left it, yet he has left it unfinished, may not appear so valuable to you, that you may think twenty-seven verses of the part that is the most finished in it, worth one and twenty hundred pounds and odd money, yet his *Georgicks*, which he put his last hand unto, will furnish you with many things far from despicable. But after all, when I said I was willing that the beauties of these two poets, might become visible to your visive faculty in poetry, I did not mean that you should judge nothing to be admittable into an

Directions for a Candidate of the Ministry

epic poem, which is not authorized by their example; but I perfectly concur with one who is inexpressibly more capable to be a judge of such a matter than I can be; that it is a false critic who with a petulant air will insult reason itself if it presumes to oppose such authority.

I proceed now to say, that if (under the guidance of a Vida) you try your young wings now and then to see what flights you can make, at least for an epigram, it may a little sharpen your sense, and polish your style, for more important performances. For this purpose you are now even overstocked with patterns, and—*Poemata passim*,[1] you may, like Nazianzen, all your days, make a little recreation of poetry in the midst of your more painful studies. Nevertheless, I cannot but advise you, withhold your throat from thirst. Be not so set upon poetry as to be always poring on the passionate and measured pages. Let not what should be sauce rather than food for you, engross all your application. Beware of a boundless and sickly appetite, for the reading of the poems, which now the rickety nation swarms withal. And let not the Circaean cup intoxicate you. But especially preserve the chastity of your soul from the dangers you may incur by a conversation with muses that are no better than harlots, among which are others besides Ovid's epistles, which for their tendency to excite and foment impure flames, and cast coals into your bosom, deserve rather to be thrown into the fire than to be laid before the eye which a covenant should be made withal. Indeed, not merely for the impurities, which they convey, but also on some other accounts, the powers of darkness have a library among us, whereof the poets have been the most numerous as well as the most venomous authors.

---

[1] Translation: "poems everywhere."

Of Poetry & Style

Most of the modern plays, as well as the romances and novels and fictions, which are a sort of poems, do belong to the catalogue of this cursed library. The plays, I say, in which there are so many passages that tend to overthrow all piety, that one whose name is Bedford, has extracted near seven thousand instances of them from the plays chiefly of but five years preceding; and says awfully upon them, they are national sins, and therefore call for national plagues. And if God should enter into judgment, all the blood in the nation would not be able to atone for them. How much do I wish that such pestilences, and indeed all those worse than Egyptian toads (the spawns of a Butler, a Brown, and a Ward, and a company whose name is Legion!) might never crawl into your chamber! The unclean spirits that come like frogs out of the mouth of the dragon, and of the beast; which go forth unto the young people of the earth, and expose them to be dealt withal as the enemies of God in the battle of the great Day of the Almighty. As for those wretched scribbles of madmen, my son, touch them not, taste them not, handle them not: you will perish in the using of them. They are the dragons whose contagious breath peoples the dark retreats of death. To much better purpose will an excellent but an envied Blackmore feast you than those vile rhapsodies (of that *Vinum daemonum*) which you will find always leave a taint upon your mind, and among other ill effects, will sensibly indispose you to converse with the holy oracles of God your Savior.

But there is, what I may rather call a parenthesis than a digression, which this may be not altogether an improper place for the introducing of.

Of style

There has been a deal of a do about a style; so much, that I must offer you my sentiments upon it. There is a way of writing, wherein the author endeavors that the reader may have something to the purpose in every paragraph. There is not only a vigor sensible in every sentence, but the paragraph is embellished with profitable references, even to something beyond what is directly spoken. Formal and painful quotations are not studied; yet all that could be learned from them is insinuated. The writer pretends not unto reading, yet he could not have written as he does if he had not read very much in his time; and his composures are not only a cloth of gold, but also stuck with as many jewels, as the gown of a Russian ambassador. This way of writing has been decried by many, and is at this day more than ever so, for the same reason, that in the old story, the grapes were decried, that they were not ripe. A lazy, ignorant, conceited set of authors would persuade the whole tribe to lay aside that way of writing, for the same reason that one would have persuaded his brethren to part with the encumbrance of their bushy rails.

But however fashion and humor may prevail, they must not think that the club at their coffee-house is all the world; but there will always be those who will, in this case, be governed by indisputable reason: and who will think that the real excellency of a book will neverly in saying of little; that the less one has for his money in a book, it is really the more valuable for it; and that the less one is instructed in a book, and the more of superfluous margin, and superficial harangue, and the less of substantial matter one has in it, the more 'tis to be accounted of. And if a more massy way of writing be never so much disgusted

Of Poetry & Style

at this day, a better gust will come on, as will some other things, *quae jam cecidere*.[2]

In the meantime, nothing appears to me more impertinent and ridiculous than the modern way (I cannot say, *rule*; for they have none!) of criticizing. The blades that set up for critics, I know not who constituted or commissioned them!—they appear to me, for the most part, as contemptible as they are a supercilious generation. For indeed no two of them have the same style; and they are as intolerably cross-grained and severe in their censures upon one another, as they are upon the rest of mankind. But while each of them, conceitedly enough, sets up for the standard of perfection, we are entirely at a loss which fire to follow. Nor can you easily find any one thing wherein they agree for their style, except perhaps a perpetual care to give us jejune and empty pages, without such touches of erudition (to speak in the style of an ingenious traveler) as may make the discourses less tedious, and more enriching to the mind of him that peruses them. There is much talk of a florid style, obtaining among the pens, that are most in vogue; but how often would it puzzle one, even with the best glasses to find the flowers! And if they were to be chastised for it, it would be with much what as much of justice, as Jerome was for being a Ciceronian. After all, every man will have his own style, which will distinguish him as much as his gate. And if you can attain to that which I have newly described, but always writing so as to give an easy conveyance unto your ideas, I would not have you by any scourging be driven out of your gate, but if you must confess a fault in it, make a confession like that of the lad, unto his father while he was beating him for his versifying.

---

[2] Translation: "which now have fallen."

However, since every man will have his own style, I would pray that we may learn to treat one another with mutual civilities and condescensions, and handsomely indulge one another in this, as gentlemen do in other matters.

I wonder what ails people that they can't let Cicero write in the style of Cicero, and Seneca write in the (much other!) style of Seneca; and own that both may please in their several ways. But I will freely tell you; what has made me consider the humorists that set up for critics upon style, as the most unregardable set of mortals in the world, is this! Far more illustrious critics than any of those to whom I am now bidding defiance, and no less men than your Erasmus's and your Grotius's have taxed the Greek style of the New Testament with I know not what solaecisms and barbarisms; and, how many learned folks have obsequiously run away with the notion! Whereas it is an ignorant and an insolent whimsy, which they have been guilty of. It may be (and particularly by an ingenious Blackwall, it has been) demonstrated that the gentlemen are mistaken in every one of their pretended instances; all the unquestionable classics, may be brought in to convince them of their mistakes. Those glorious oracles are as pure Greek as ever was written in the world; and so correct, so noble, so sublime is their style, that never anything under the cope of heaven, but the Old Testament, has equaled it.

9
NATURAL PHILOSOPHY

What we call *natural philosophy* is what I must encourage you to spend much more time in the study of.

Do it with continual contemplations and agreeable acknowledgements of the infinite God, whose perfections are so displayed in His works before you, that from them you cannot but be perpetually ravished into the acclamations of how great is His goodness and His beauty!

Do it with a design to be led into those views wherewith you will in ways most worthy of a man effectually. Show yourself a man, and may with unutterable satisfaction answer the main end of your being, which is: to glorify God; and therein also discharge the office of a priest for the creation; which, how sweet a token for good must it be unto you!

When I said, natural philosophy, you may be sure, I did not mean, the Peripatetic: for I heartily subscribe to the censure of *Christianus Thomasius* upon it; *omne tempus pro perdito judicandum, quod in physicam peripateticorum impenditur; ita inepta et stulta ibi sunt omnia.*[1] It is indeed amazing to see the fate of the writings which go under the name of Aristotle. First, falling

---

[1] Translation: "For all time what depends on the on the philosophy of the Peripatetics must be regarded as loss, so inept and stupid are all things in that place."

into the hands of those who could not read them, and yet for the sake of the famous author were willing to keep them; they were for a long while hid underground, where many of them deserved a lodging. And from this place of darkness the torn or worn manuscripts were anon fetched out; and imperfectly and unfaithfully enough transcribed, and conveyed from Athens to Rome, where copies were in like manner taken of them. The Saracens at last got them, and (the concise and broken style a little suiting them) they spoke Arabic; and even in Africa there were many Aristotelean schools erected. They were from thence brought over into Spain, and exhibited with such translations and commentaries as it pleased the Arabians to bestow upon them. When learning revived under Charlemagne, all Europe turned Aristotelean; yea, in some universities they swore allegiance to him; and, O monstrous! if I am not misinformed, they do in some universities at this day foolishly and profanely on their knees continue to do so. With the vile person that made himself the head of the Church at Rome, this muddy-headed Pagan divided the Empire over the Christian world; but extended his Empire further than he, or ever any Tamerlane. For the very Jews themselves became his vassals, with a tradition of his having some relation to, or at least some acquaintance with, their fathers. And though Europe has, with fierce and long struggles about it, begun to shake off the shackles, he does to this day, under the name of Aplis, continue to tyrannize over humane understanding in a great part of the Oriental world.

No mortal else ever had such a prerogative to govern mankind as this philosopher, who after the prodigious cartloads of stuff that has been written to explain him (For within a few centuries after Albertus Magnus, there were twelve-thousand authors that wrote upon him; or followed him and defended him; and by a probable computation, there have since been more than as many more!). He yet remains in many other things besides his Entelechia sufficiently unintelligible, and forever in almost all things unprofitable. Avicen, after he had read his *Metaphysics* forty times over and had them all by heart, was forced after all to lay them aside, in despair of ever understanding them. Have done, then, with your Magirus, and your Eustachius, and your Heereboord; and the rest of the jargon-writers. Just so far as to see a little what they say, you may look into them; whatsoever is more, cometh of evil, and evil will come of it.

Some eminent persons, besides a Sennertus and a Valesius, tired with the academic futilities, have at length betaken themselves to the best school for philosophy as well as for theology. The Mosaic philosophy in the scheme that Comenius has given of it, is much admired and embraced in some reformed universities; and you will do well to bestow a deliberate reading upon it. The *Philosophia Vetus ac Vera* of the rare Dickinson has given us a yet finer piece of Mosaic work, which must always be honorably spoken of. But, though it be true that the Sacred Scriptures have a wondrous philosophy in them, and a memorable Dutchman has lately demonstrated, that, according to what every day makes more and more evident, the prophetic spirit from whose inspiration they are given to us, knew and owned, the now most undisputed things which occur in the discoveries of our modern philosophy. Yet it is now plain, the first chapter of Genesis (as well as the rest of the Bible, which refers to the system of the world), has not been well understood by most of the gentlemen that have written upon it. However, because of the regard therein paid unto Moses,

DIRECTIONS FOR A CANDIDATE OF THE MINISTRY

and *The Traduction of our Philosophy from the Holy Fountains* (though Plato be advanced with him), I do particularly approve your perusing of the *Philosophia generalis*, written by our equally modest and learned Gale, so as to make yourself a master of it. I cannot but confess that the hypotheses which the more ingenious and inquisitive sons of the wild ass's colt have hitherto mostly valued themselves upon, have been too justly called "Philosophical Romances," and it may be, what is now most in vogue, may anon be refuted and refused like its predecessors. Nevertheless, I would have you take what may appear least likely to prove romantic. And therefore, as thorough an insight as you can get into the principles of our perpetual dictator, the incomparable Sir Isaac Newton is what I mightily commend unto you.

Be sure, the experimental philosophy is that in which alone your mind can be at all established. For this purpose, besides your more occasionally conversing with such things as, our philosophical transactions, and several communications of our illustrious Boyl, and of Hook, and of Grew, and Cheyne, and Keill, and those also that have written the natural history of several places (and such outlandish writings as those of Bartholinus, and Borellus, and the German Ephemerides); I would commend unto you, *The Religious Philosopher*, of the Admirable Nieuentyt; and what has been communicated by our industrious Ray, and our ingenuous Derham, who still nobly serve religion as well as philosophy. And whatever it might be for me to say so unto anyone else, I hope, it will be no indecency for me to say so unto you; that if you desire to see the largest collection, I have yet seen of the discoveries which the last age has made in philosophy, adapted unto the general capacity of readers; and short essays upon every article, to show and raise those dispositions of piety, wherein the works of the holy and blessed God invite us to live unto Him; together with the first claim that I have ever yet seen so explicitly made on the behalf of a glorious Christ, and the consideration due to him in our philosophy; you have this prepared for you in a book entitled, *The Christian Philosopher*.[2]

Above all, I would have you see to it that you be not, like some haughty, and short-sighted, and half-witted, smatterers in philosophy, seduced into the folly of doubting the existence or providence of a Glorious God by a study, which, if well-pursued, would compel you to come in to a strong faith, wherewith you would give glory to Him on all occasions. I hope, every step of your study will give you more and more satisfaction, of what one of our best philosophers, the author of *The Natural History of the Earth*, adheres unto: "That as the world was at first created, so it has been ever since preserved by the immediate hand of God." You will see that the influences of one thing upon another in the course of nature are purely from the omnipotent and omnipresent God, actually forever at work, according to His own laws, and putting His laws in execution, and as the universal cause producing those effects, whereof the creatures are but what one may call, "the occasional causes." You will also be often and quickly carried up into those immechanical principles, from whence, the next step is into God! The gravitation of bodies is one of them, for which no cause can be assigned, but the will of the Glorious God, who is the first cause of all.

Child, see God in everything! Own Him, fear Him, love Him; study philosophy with a perpetual intention to do so.

---

[2] Cotton Mather's *The Christian Philosopher* (1721) was the first systematic science book published in America.

Remember, God is to spirits what center is to bodies. And a mind that, from the view of the Glorious God in His works, is carried into acknowledgements of a God infinitely worthy to be loved and praised and served and relied upon, becomes a temple filled with the glory of the Lord. Visit for this purpose the several classes of the creatures. Walk through the world (and be so far a peripatetic!); and in this generous exercise, fear God and give glory unto Him.

10
MATHEMATICS

The mathematics will be, next unto philosophy, a noble study for you; the most essential parts whereof you have in the *Cursus Mathematicus* of an Ozanam so delivered unto you, that indeed you will hardly need anymore. Though you are shaping for a divine, yet I should not be sorry to see you as exquisite a mathematician as the excellent Pitiscus who, though he were a divine, yet without a tutor became such an high attainer in this real learning, that Melchior Adam cries out, *Illud mirandum!*[1] upon it: And it caused the noble Tycho Brahe to say, *Optarem plures ejusmodi concionatores reperiri: forte plus esset in iis circumspecti et solidi judicii.*[2] I should not be sorry to see a Wallis, or a Wilkins, or a Barrow, revived in you, if your genius led you to it.

Arithmetic & geometry
Besides the other uses of *arithmetic* and *geometry*, (wherein an Hill and an Euclid, or, *The Young Mathematicians Guide of a Ward*, instead of both, may singularly be commended), you will

---

[1] Translation: "That's amazing!"
[2] Translation: "I would that more demagogues of this sort be found. Perhaps there would be more circumspect and solid judgment in them."

Directions for a Candidate of the Ministry

find this benefit by the study of them; they will necessitate and habituate your mind unto that strong attention, which will marvelously qualify you for more important services, make a strong reasoner of you, and a very regular and coherent speaker. They were distinguished by the name of "mathesis," and made the first learning in some ancient schools, for this very reason. And you may be sure, I should reckon it a further encouragement unto the study, if the general rule might hold without any exception that great mathematicians use to be men of good morals; it seems that their intense applications and speculations are inconsistent with debaucheries. While you are thus employed, methinks, it might be a pretty diversion to go through some of Leybourn's *Mathematical Recreations*.

Astronomy

But you must also soar upwards to the attainments of *astronomy*. For though, of later ages, the voluminous Tostatus, whom they complemented as having all the learning in the world, were no better an astronomer than Justin Martyr, and Ambrose, and Theodoret, and Chrysostom, and Austin himself, who in the more early ages declaimed violently against the spherical figure of the heavens; I should be loth you should through ignorance in astronomy, ever fall into what even a Jerome would call *Stultiloquium in ecclesia*.[3] Wherefore, I cannot but advise you to be well instructed in the astronomical lectures, as of an accurate Keill, so of the acute Whiston; while we are mourning, that he who so excellently serves us in astronomy should so unhappily hurt us in divinity and call into question (as a dubious problem) the infinite and eternal Godhead of

---

[3] Translation: "Babbling in church."

Him *for* whom, as well as *by* whom, the sun and the stars were created.

Judicial astrology

At the same time, I hope, there is no need of my saying anything to dissuade you from the study of *judicial astrology*: The most injudicious thing in the world: All futility; all impiety; all of a piece with the ridiculous whim of a Gaffarel, who maintains that the stars in the heavens do stand ranged in the form of Hebrew letters, and that it is possible to read there whatever is to happen of importance throughout the universe. And yet, perhaps, there may be some need for me to caution you against being dismayed at the signs of the heavens, or having any superstitious fancies upon eclipses and the like occurrences, or thinking that if there were a conjunction of all the planets in Pisces, it would portend that the world should be drowned. Yea, I am willing that the cometomancy which has hitherto so much reigned, even in the most honest minds, be laid aside with you; and that you be apprehensive of nothing portentous in blazing stars, except it should be apprehended, that in their elliptic motions they may make so near an appulse unto this globe as to bring some confusion upon it. For my part, I know not whether all our worlds, and even the sun itself may not fare the better for them. Some, that know more than I, do think so. Indeed, if you persuade a world, here lying in wickedness, there to see a presage, and to take a warning from the tremendous view of a world in a state of punishment, I will say, go on and prosper.

DIRECTIONS FOR A CANDIDATE OF THE MINISTRY

Geography

But I will now so far fetch you down from the stars, and set you down on your native soil as to tell you, that there is nothing mathematical to which I more advise you than the easy study of *geography*. Perhaps the situation of Paradise and of Palestine and of the places mentioned in the Sacred Scriptures, may be what you would be willing to be first of all acquainted with. And for this, let the admirable Bochart be your principal instructor. What has been chiefly taken from him, and from two or three more, in three or four Octavo's under the title of *Sacred Geography* (by one Wells) may herein also be of some use to you. *The Pisgah Sight* of a Fuller will be read with a pleasure equal to the profit; and the *Palestina Illustrata* of a Reland, perhaps with a profit greater than the pleasure. But you will not give over till more of the world has come into your knowledge, than the decree of an Augustus could reach unto.

Wherefore, after a Morden or a Gordon (together with a Varenius) has given you a more compendious view of the world, I say nothing of a work entitled, *Geography Rectified*, because 'tis not easy to find a work that more wants to be rectified; but what I say next, is, that the *Atlas Geographus*, will be a yet more instructive guide for you in your taking the tour of the several regions in it. You may, then, as your inclinations may carry you, with delight and safety make your visits to particular countries and cities, in the descriptions given of them. And here, while I suppose that what a Camden has given you in his *Britannia*, will be no unacceptable entertainment for you, I cannot but notify it unto you, that, *The English Empire in America* described by one Oldmixon, is the most foolish and faithless performance in this kind that ever mankind was abused withal.

MATHEMATICS

I am desirous that you proceed and peruse many of the travels that have been published; and (if you dare not venture upon a purchase) by conversing with many more than what are exhibited in that rich collection which goes under the name of, *Itinerantium atque navigantium bibliotheca*,[4] you may with little expense or hazard become a notable traveler. In your thus riding a circuit, you will especially inform yourself about the state of religion in the world: (And methinks, Paget's *Christianography*, and Brierwood's *Enquiries*, may particularly deserve a reading with you). And you will have your heart thereupon raised in sentiments of gratitude unto a sovereign God, who has cast your lot among a people whom He has known above most of the families of the earth: even so Righteous Father, for so it pleases Thee!—and compassion for a world over so much of which the powers of darkness continue to tyrannize: disposed like an owner of Seller's *New System of Geography*, whom I found inserting with his pen this note at the end of it: *Peccantis et perditi tam, vasti mundi, miserere Deus!*[5] Yea, in fine, let me tell you, this easy study will not only furnish you to maintain a profitable conversation, and a communication that may minister grace, and be ever acceptable to the hearers: but if you prove a man of concern for the kingdom of God in the world, it may bring you to form those projections, by which, as little as you are in your own eyes, whole nations may anon come to fare the better for you.

---

[4] Translation: "Library of Land and Sea Voyages."
[5] Translation: "God pity the sinner and the lost of such a vast world."

Music

For *music*, I know not what well to say—do as you please. If you fancy it, I don't forbid it. Only do not for the sake of it alienate your time too much from those that are more important matters. It may be so that you may serve your God the better for the refreshment of one that can play well on an instrument. However, to accomplish yourself at regular singing is a thing that will be of daily use to you. For I would not have a day pass you without singing, but so as at the same time to make a melody in your heart unto the Lord; besides the part you may bear, *In Hymnis suavisonantis ecclesiae.*[6]

I will conclude this article with a remark made by Perault in his account of *Illustrious Men.* Some reproached Gassendus for not knowing enough certain parts of the mathematics. Whereupon he says:

> Whether he was actually ignorant of what was most abstruse in these sciences, or whether he neglected it, he could not but be the more commendable for it. There is something of little, in tying oneself up too much to little things; and even of imprudence too, to consume therein a time, which may be employed more usefully on other knowledge.

---

[6] Translation: "In hymns making a sweet sound in the church."

11
STUDY & USE OF HISTORY

If the Emperor Basil had not, in his *Instructions to a Son*, recommended unto him history as a way of traveling without fatigue, you may be sure, my son, that I should have recommended unto you an acquaintance with history as one of the most needful and useful accomplishments for a man that would serve God as you propose to do. The praises of that method which they that handle the pen of the writer have taken to stop the flood of things, and give a consistency and a duration unto them, that historians usually begin their works withal, and the flourishes about, *Lux Veritatis, Vita Memoriae, Magistra Vitae*.[1] And I know not what are as unnecessary on this occasion, as they are on that whereon we commonly have them. And though perhaps we cannot meet with such historians as Le Moyne pleases to require, but such as he says, will not appear until the year when the Philosopher's Stone shall be discovered. Yet I would not have you discouraged from reading the best we have.

---

[1] Translation: "The light of truth, the life of memory, the teacher of life" (Cicero, *De Oratore*, 2.36).

General history

But for this purpose, I shall be far from advising you to impose on yourself the tedious task of reading over the hundreds of histories, which Degory Whear or the Frenchman who has more lately written, *L'Histoire des Histoires*, may obtrude upon you. Except you were to have the long life of an Antediluvian; and even then also to read them all would be to spend much time impertinently. Perhaps a concise body of universal history may be very properly laid in the foundation of your historical studies. And though Hornius' *Arca Noae* be admirable, and Sleidan's little book, *De quatuor summis Imperiis* be far from despicable, yet I can't presently think of a better than Matthias Prideaux's easy and compendious *Introduction* for the reading all sorts of histories. Proceed, then, to some volume of larger dimensions, among which I can tell of none that I could more heartily commend unto you than Howel's *Institution of General History*. And upon this, add Pussendorf's *Introduction*. But I will here betimes lay in for this: in reading of all history, every now and then, make a convenient pause to think: what can I see of the Glorious God in these occurrences? And always remember, the providence of the Glorious God in governing the world is now under my contemplation.

Doubtless you will have a desire, if you can find a leisure, to read some histories of particular countries. And here, as I know none better than Mezeray, for France; Mariana, for Spain; Grotius, for Holland; Knoles with Rycaut, for the Ottoman Empire; Ludolphus, for Abyssinia; Crull, for Russia (there are several small storytellers for Persia and Indoustan), Martinius, and some other Jesuits (but you must remember, they are Jesuits!) for China; Martyr, or Acosta, or Ogilby, for America; Buchanan, for Scotland; and Cox for Ireland. So, I

USE OF HISTORY

would prefer Baker, for England; especially, if you could come at an edition that was printed before what they call, "The Restoration." *The Memorials of English Affairs*, from the supposed Expedition of Brute into the Island, until the coming of King James I. (doesn't something in the title sound a little odd?) written by Whitlock, or the little, *Medulla Historiae Angelicanae*, may also be to you a pretty abstract of our English history.

But the mention of English affairs pushes me, even with some anticipation, into the caution which I am to give you about reading all our common histories; but none more than the English ones, that is, to believe with discretion. Alas, the vanity which attends human affairs! As there are many men and things that are scarce mentioned in true history which deserve a mention more than some that are universally celebrated; what heroes are buried among those who lived before the Days of Agamemnon? And Walter Plettenberg is less known than a Turkish pyrate: what has been ponderous has (as my Lord Bacon expresses it) been sunk to the bottom in the stream of time, while we have straw and stubble swimming a top. So, 'tis a thing that may be too truly, but can't be too sadly complained of, that the instances wherein false history has been imposed upon the world are what cannot be numbered. Historians have generally taken after their father, Herodotus. And even one of themselves, Vopiscus by name, has expressly said of them, "They are all them liars: this witness is true!" Though they have not all of them always been such mercenary villains as Bishop Jovius, or that scandalous fellow who more lately so hired himself out as an history writer for the highest bidder, that his countrymen, the Italians, fixed that motto on him. Not according to the history but the salary; yet one who

Directions for a Candidate of the Ministry

gently enough criticizes on them too justly questions whether any modern historian has thought of any more than pleasing the prince or party for which he wrote.

The ancients are not much better than the modern, whereof we have a notorious and amazing example in Josephus. It would be too long a digression to relate his vile prevarications, which have compelled us to concur unto the censure passed by our Gregory upon him, that being ambitious to have his work find acceptance among the heathen, he did so compose his history as to propose nothing that might appear incredible to them, and not have some congruity with what had been, and was likely again to be among them. Indeed all honest men are scandalized, no less than Castrius, at the pains he takes to make his court unto the Roman princes by his heathen Judaism; wherein, as one says, he was more impious than the Philistines who placed the Ark by Dagon.

What a fine story are we like to have of as infamous a reign as ever was in the world, and a tyranny all made up of treacheries and robberies and cruelties that cannot be paralleled, when it comes from three poets, each of them with a pension of twelve thousand livres a year, to give us a panegyric instead of an history, and outdo a Paterculus blanching his Tiberius! How little many representations of matters in histories are to be relied upon, methinks, it may be a little illustrated from the two chief commanders in a memorable Battle of Belgrade, both of which, wrote the history of the battle without the least mention made by the one of the other each assuming to himself the entire honor of the day. You will certainly say: "Who can understand his Errors?"—When the admirable Erasmus himself mistakes one man for two in writing of what was a great while ago, and three professed and eminent historians give us a very wrong account of the gentleman who a much less while ago founded the Charter-House; and though no writer of history ever were more meritorious than the incomparable Thuanus; yet learned men have said of his performance, that it contained *Multa falsissima et indigna.*[2]

Yea, there are historians of whom one can scarce tell which to admire most, the nature of their lies, or their manner of telling them. I mean, the impudence with which they tell them. For instance, it is pretty well that Hozier the French king's *Genealogift* has discovered no less than four thousand wrong things in *Varillas*, the same King's Historian. And another observes, every single page in him has almost as many errors as a printer's ordinary table of errata. But then, what an impudent fellow was Philanax Anglicus, when he accused Calvin of delicacy and Epicureanism in his way of living, and quotes Florimond de Remond for a witness of it, who, he says, "has left us a lively image of him." Whereas, if you consult this Florimond de Remond, the lively image which he gives of Calvin is that, "from his youth he macerated his body with fasting, and that hardly could be found a man that equaled him for his laboriousness." Be sure, the late historians that pretend unto a history of England for us write with such flagrant partialities, and are such evident leasing-makers, and palm upon you so very wrong and base exhibitions, especially of late occurrences, that one may as well believe the true history of a Lucian, as yield any credit unto them.

If you must read them, yet as to things that passed in the former century, I would hardly so much as look upon many of them. And among these, though several are bad enough, yet

---

[2] Translation: "Many things most false and unworthy."

there is none that has done so ill as an Eachard (I mean, in his English, and not in his Roman history), who should not be admitted into the library of a gentleman that has any concern for truth; except he'll assign him a place on the same shelf with the Grand Cyrus or Cleopatra. A late critical history of England has done some justice upon him. Indeed, the historians never keep closer to the way of lying than in the relation they give of those twenty years which passed after the beginning of our Civil Wars, and afforded a very ample and fertile field for their faculty to work upon. Among these, the romance that goes under the title of *The History of the Grand Rebellion*, and is fathered on the Earl of Charendon, I would have you more particularly treat with the disregard that is proper for it.

If you would come at all near to the truth of what concerns those times, you must look for it in Whitlock's *Memorials of English Affairs*, from the beginning of King Charles I to the restoring of King Charles II. And Rushworth's *Collections*. And yet even there, some of the greatest persons and actions have not always full justice done them. I do particularly advertise you that the mighty man, whom not only our King William (as Fleming reports) had a very high esteem for, but also his most bigoted and bitterest enemies confess to have been a matchless hero, and (as even Sr. Roger Manly himself, as well as many more of his Bran, acknowledges) not unworthy of the supreme heighth of empire which he attained to has never yet had his history fairly and fully given. And when you read it given (as they are now approaching towards it) with the greatest impartiality wherein you have hitherto seen it, you may bear this in your mind that the principal stroke in his character, and the principal spring of his conduct, is forever defectively related.

Use of History

As for such abominable pens as what the *Athenae Oxonienses* of a Wood have been excretions from, you cannot sufficiently despise them and abhor them. And I will further tell you that if in any history you happen to find any vindicating or favorable passages of old Archbishop Laud, let these be Shibboleth enough with you, to do the office which the rattle does for the serpent, which our country is no stranger to. Yea, and when you read, even such conscientious historians as a Baxter and a Burnet, you must make allowances for some hearsays, which led them into mistakes; and for certain prejudices, the tincture whereof a little influenced their views of what they were disaffected to.

Church history

Having thus armed you for a walk among the woods of civil history, I must now propose Church History with a yet more earnest wish to have you well-acquainted with it. For although Grotius observes, *Qui legit Historiam Ecclesiasticam, quid legit, nisi Episcoporum Vitia?*[3] And others have been so satirical as to say, "Ecclesiastical history is nothing but many large volumes, containing some few of the squabbles of the bishops and inferior clergy with one another and all the world." Nevertheless a divine has a blemish upon him almost as disqualifying as any of the hundred-and-forty, which the Jews reckon to bring a priest of theirs under incapacities, if church history has not instructed him for the business of the sanctuary.

Now, for a regular system of church history, I know not that I can tender you a better than Spanheim's *Introductio ad*

---

[3] Translation: "The one who reads church history, what does he read, except the faults of the bishops?"

Historiam et Antiquitates Sacras. To which, by all means, add Hornius' *Historia Ecclesiastica,* and Usher's *De Christianarum Ecclesrarum Successione et Statu.* If you would have what is English and easy, 'tis done to your hand by a Scotchman, that is to say, Patrick Simpson in his *History of the Church.* Somewhat larger than these and never enough to be commended is Hottinger's, *Historia Ecclesiastica Novi Testamenti.* But then, I would have you, if you don't wholly peruse, yet by all means possess and often visit, the *Ecclesiastical History* of the Magdeburgensian Centuriators; of which noble work I will say what Spanheim said before me; that it is *Bibliotheca totius Christianae Antiquitatis — incredibili cum Studio, Fide optima, Meth do utilissima, congesta.*[4]

There have been also more particular essays of church history, which you may do well to find some time for conversation with. Such more especially are what we have had from Eusebius, whom they call "The Father of Church History;" together with, *The Tripartite History* of Socrates, and Theodoret, and Sozomen, continued by Evagrius. As a kind of a postscript, whereunto you can scarce read a more profitable thing than Vedelius' *Prudentia Veteris Ecclesiae.* But you may prudently join with it Millar's *History of the Propagation of Christianity.* And with how much edification run over, Illyricus' *Catalogus Testium Veritatis*! Coming lower down, I am fond of your familiarity with a book very little known among us; 'tis Regenvolscius' *Systema Historico-Chronologicum Ecclesiarum Sclavonicarum.* But you will do well also to read Sleidan's Commentaries; Moreland's *History of the Waldenses*; Calderwood's

---

[4] Translation: "A library of the whole of Christian antiquity, filled with incredible study, extremely trustworthy, and of the most useful method."

USE OF HISTORY

Church-History of Scotland; Fuller's *Church-History of England*, and Burnet's *History of the Reformation*. Therein, make wise reflections on the providence of Him who has all power in Heaven and Earth for the upholding of His Kingdom in the world.

Nor should our martyrologies be left unconsulted. But in them you will behold the cup given to Christ mystical in the sufferings of His faithful people; and admire the operations of the Spirit that strengthened the sufferers with such patience and such fortitude: the grace given to the children of men! As for the histories of Councils; if Angelocrator's brief *Epitome Conciliorum* do not content you, I cannot wish you to go beyond Coriolanus. The more elephantine books of them, I won't so much as give you the titles. But instead of them, I pray read Baxter's *Church-History of the Government of Bishops and their Councils*. Nevertheless, *The History of the Council of Trent*, and the *Acta* of the Synod of Dort. I could be glad if you could give some winter evenings to. And what an illustrious person has offered as a king upon, *The Discipline of the Primitive Church* and *The History of the Creed*, must by no means be forgotten in the visits of your studies.

But Cicero is not the only gentleman who has been able to say that, in history they have especially studied the portraiture of wise men "who have been before them, to imprint on themselves as far as might be the resemblance of them." I hope you will do so too; and read the lives, especially of them who have done worthily in Israel, not only on the intention of rendering praises to the Glorious God who did such things as you will see done *for* and *by* these notable men, but also intending in as many points as may be, to *go* and *do* likewise. Be sure that whenever you see greatness and goodness and brightness in any excellent person whose life you have in your hands, you look off to the Glorious Jesus, as having in Him all these excellencies after a transcendent manner, and as being the Author and Giver of them to the distinguished glow worm. And when you read of any imitable piety in any of them, think with yourself:

> The virtues of this man were first Jesus that called him into this marvelous light, and from Him it was derived unto this believer. O my Savior, let me also feel such influences of Thy Holy Spirit as may change me into the same image from glory to glory!

More particularly, there are two little Octavo's entitled, *Biographia Ecclesiastica*, or *The Lives of the most Eminent Fathers of the Christian Church*, which you must needs make yourself owner of. And if you go into cave, his *Lives of the Fathers*, you will be well entertained there. The *Lives* written by Melchior Adam may be very edifying for the Latin as well as the matter of them. So are the *Vitae Selectorum aliquot Virorum*, which one (they say, a Bates) has bound up in a bundle for us. In Witten's *Memoriae Renovatae*, you may ever now and then find an oration which an hour will not be unprofitably thrown away that shall be afforded to. Indeed, Freberns' *Theatrum* has in it such an abbreviation of *Lives* that his pictures will give you almost as much pleasure as his accounts of them that have been men of renown in the congregation of the learned. Yet I can tell you of theatres much less worthy to be gone unto. And though there hardly ever was a more dull and lifeless transcriber than our S. Clark, yet in the Collections of *Lives* that go under his name, there are very many highly worthy, not only your considering of, but also your conforming to them. And you may read his Collections with another sort of reliance than you can the

USE OF HISTORY

romances of a Simeon Metaphrastes, whom even a Baronius himself is ashamed of. Of the many *Lives* that have been published since those Collections, there are so many which you won't be either weary or the worse for casting your eye upon, that if I should go to tell you which, I shall tire you with too long a catalogue. If I should enter upon it, I hope I should steer clear of Bellarmine's disingenuity, for which our Prideaux well taxes him, who in his *Book of Ecclesiastical Writers* has not the honesty to name one of our side. But I would encourage you to read the *Life* of a William Burkitt, as well as of a Philip Henry; and what you have in Fuller's *Worthies of England*, and what a Walton has collected, as well as what you have in the Life of a Guthry, an Angier, a Flavel, and a Dorney; a Dr. More, as well as a Dr. Manton; a Dr. Horneck, as well as well as a Dr. Owen. I had left unmentioned the *Parentator*,[5] which gives the Life of Dr. [Increase] Mather, if the old usage it has met withal had not compelled me to mention it. But now I have reason more than ever to say, let that history be taken in among those that (particularly for variety) may have some consideration with you.

In fine: 'Tis possible you may find a church history wherein the *Lives* of good men may be the most significant ingredients of the composition. If you do, I wish you the satisfaction of time well spent in such harmless company.

I have nothing to add, but that you must have the clock of time set right with you by Chronology if you would be an understanding traveler in history. For the Chronology of the Bible, I can refer you to none so well as to a Whiston, whose decisive searches do supersede all the trouble of repairing to those who have writ before him. And for the Chronology of all

---

[5] This is Cotton's own biography of his father, Increase Mather (1724).

ages, our Tallents has by his *Tables* prepared such a feast for you that you will have little need of repairing to any other quarter. An Usher, a Calvisius, a Baily, will enrich your library; and it may be worth your while to have them at hand upon occasion. But for a daily recourse, you can have nothing at hand more expeditious or more comprehensive than the *Thesaurus Chronologiae* of the gentleman whose name was very truly anagrammatized into Sedulitas; in which quality I wish you may make a pattern of him.

That your library may be furnished with a magazine of history to which you may continually go for everything that your mind may lead you to, the *Theatrum Humanae Vitae* of a Zuinger in the last and large edition is one of the best that I can advise you to. For occasional readings, you may do well to divert yourself with Camerarius' *Horae Subcesivae*; with Prideaux's *Connection*; and with such things as Wanly's *History of Man*; and Cambden's *Remains*. I would have added Montfaucon's *Antiquities Explained*, if I could have told you how to come at so costly a collection. But I may add Lewis's Hebrew, Kennet's Roman, and Potter's *Greek Antiquities* as worthy your having and reading.

But for a yet more immense treasure of history and of all that belongs unto it, Hofman has a Lexicon for you in four stately folios, which alone may be called a library. The Great Historical Dictionary now appearing in English, has been growing from Stephens's Time, through the hands of Loyd and Moreri, and others, till at last, an odd man by hurting and mangling of it, and making some additions (whereof many are none of the best) unto it has obtained that it must go under the name of Collier—a fate quite the reverse of what has befallen Calepine. It should with all its faults be in your library; but

USE OF HISTORY

then, *The Critical History* of Bayle, if you can be enriched with it, will not only correct many of the faults in that, but also be for you almost another library. 'Tis a Work to be wondered at! Only guard against the Manichaean Sophistry, sometimes appearing in it.

And here it may be a proper time for me to say: when you see such astonishing effects of erudition and application produced from the sons of men, as you will find in some that have been (and others that might be) mentioned, let the sight still produce from you some due acknowledgements of the Glorious God: "My God, I adore Thy power, Thy wisdom, Thy goodness, conspicuous in these wonderful performances!"

But for the close of all, I will give you this one hint of a more general importance. There are books which, for the grateful stores of learning amassed in them, I can't but wish that you would in the parentheses of your studies often repair unto. Those which among these, I would more particularly single out for a recommendation to you are the *De Veritate Religionis Christianae* of a Grotius, *The Demonstratio Evangelica* of a Huetius, *The Theologoumena* of an Owen, everything of an admirable Hospinian, or Heidegger, *The Apology* of an Hakewel, The *Miscellanea* and *Meletemata* of a Witsius, Parker on the Cross, Basnage's *History of the Jews*; adding the *Origines Sacrae* of a Stillingfleet, the *Court of the Gentiles* of a Gale, and the *Antiquitates Biblicae* of a Dietenious.

12
SOME USEFUL PROPOSALS TO STUDENTS

Even while you are yet in your early youth, and but in your course towards the fair havens of theology, at which I am now quickly to land you, I would advise to two things whereof you will certainly find an inexpressible and almost incredible advantage.

Keep a quotidiana

One thing that I advise you to is this: Keep your Quotidiana.[1] I mean, have your blank books in which note with your pen for the most part every day. Let there be, *Nulla Dies sine Linea!*[2] — Some notable thing which, in reading, you have newly met withal. By this action you will fix the valuable notion in your mind. And in a few years, you will have a treasure from whence as a scribe instructed for the Kingdom of Heaven, you may bring out things new and old, and have agreeable grains of salt for all your discourses. You will not for this use the unequal way of entering the riches of your Quotidiana in pages with the titles of a commonplace at the tops of them, whereof some will be soon crammed and others remain empty, perhaps all your days. But enter the things as they come, with only affixing the number to them. And have at the end of the books an

---

[1] Mather kept a journal for random thoughts and musings which he called his "Quotidiana."

[2] Translation: "No day without an entry!"

alphabetical index of the matter with the number at which it is to be met withal. Here you will anon have an inexhaustible magazine. And if you live to old age, you will find that, like old Photius, you have prepared a hive then to live upon. I will not say you will be quickly as rich as Craesus, for poor Craesus will have no riches comparable to what you will have in your collections.

Form a sodality
Another thing that I advise you to is this: form a *Sodality*. What I mean is, prevail with a fit number (six or seven may be a competency, or fewer, if you can't find so many) of sober, ingenious, and industrious young men to associate with you, and meet one evening in a week for the spending of two or three hours in a profitable conversation. At this interview, let there be always a sort of director who shall propose this question (and see that without needless digressions and excursions it be kept close unto): what remarkable and memorable matter has occurred in late studies that is thought now to be offered? Let the question be articulated, and more particularly and successively, turn upon these Articles.

I. What in Philology?
II. What in Philosophy?
III. What in Geography, and the rest of the Mathematics?
IV. What in History?
V. What in illustrations of the Sacred Scriptures; or Biblical Curiosities?

Let each person, in what order they shall agree upon, give his report as concisely as may be. But it will not be expected that each person should be prepared at every time with something on every head. It is enough that he bring in, for that cell, which he happens to be best furnished for. All altercations and all impertinencies are to be forever banished from those communications of the Sodality.

But how much could I wish that you could gain one quarter of an hour in the close of all to relate: what rare flight or fine stroke of the Christian Ascetics has been met withal; and what for the animation of practical piety? Behold, a way to clench the nails that have been struck into your minds, and a compendious and charitable course to come at the wealth, which the diligence of your brethren has made them the owners of; together with the generous pleasure of making them the partakers of yours. 'Twill have a tendency also to qualify you for useful conference in other company, and make you a speaker whose words may always be as the choicest silver, and as fruits from the Tree of Life to such as you converse withal. It was a remark that Plato made a good while ago; that the true manner of teaching sciences is by conversation. And, we never well understand a truth if we are not in a condition on all occasions to make it known unto such as are for the receiving of it.

Because of its being somewhat akin to this, and because we are just now entering upon the study of divinity, I will, though there may seem almost some anticipation in it, here transcribe a passage from the *Paterna* of one whom it may be, you are not wholly a stranger to, and who was himself but a very young man, when he was engaged in the projection referred unto:

> I singled out a number of students who had passed through their cursus in philosophical and academic studies, and were just entering into the world. These young gentlemen met once a week at my study,

where we carried on a course of disputation upon the body of divinity. In the several common place heads of divinity, where any notable controversy had been managed in the church of God, we had a solemn disputation on the controverted question. In this disputation, I was always the moderator, and still concluded with a discourse, which by argument established the truth, defended by the respondent. But, because upon every head of divinity there were multitudes of questions not so worthy of a solemn disputation. These I laboriously gathered up, and giving them to the society at some of our meetings, we came all prepared with brief but strong and proved answers to them, which we accordingly delivered in our order. The benefit of these exercises we found unspeakable!

13
Sentiments which Ministry is to Be Undertaken

All this while I have been proposing to bring you on towards the Evangelical ministry, and the study of theology for it and in it, after such a manner as to render you a skillful artist for the work of your God.

Now, surely it is not at all congruous to study divinity upon any other than divine principles. But when you are in the approaches of theology, more particularly fixing your purpose to be (if the Lord will!) a minister of the gospel, it is necessary that since you desire a good work, it may be upon a good end that you do it. Let such noble considerations as these have their influence upon you:

> A work I have now before me, wherein I am to be perpetually rendering acknowledgments to the Glorious God in enquiries for and confessions of the truths of His holy religion; and procuring acknowledgements to Him from others by acquainting them with such truths, and persuading them to that piety, which they are thereby to be led unto.
>
> A work, whereof the main and the next intention is to restore the throne of God in the soul of man, and bring the sons of death into the life of God; and into those methods of piety, wherein they will glorify God and enjoy Him forever.

Directions for a Candidate of the Ministry

A work, whereof the grand aim is to exhibit the glories of a lovely Redeemer of whom how great is the goodness and the beauty! And fill up His mystical body by bringing in to Him those whom His Father has given to Him; and whose coming under the shadow of His wings was the joy set before Him to comfort Him in His travailing agonies.

A work, which is to turn the children of men from darkness unto light, and from the power of Satan unto God, and instruct, and assist, and animate the children of God in choosing and in doing the things that please Him, and raise living temples for God, and fill them with His glory.

In fine, a work which, if done with all good fidelity, will in a future state be followed with astonishing recompenses—"Thy work shall be rewarded," saith the Lord!

Unto this work, as a work that indeed carries its own wages in it, and a work which on these illustrious accounts, no other calling may be compared unto, you will now bring yourself under a most solemn dedication. With a heart marvelously set upon this work of God, humbly thus declare unto Him:

Glorious God, owning myself utterly unworthy of such a favor, I desire to devote myself unto the Service of my Savior; and I entreat of Thee graciously to accept of me. Sensible that I can do nothing, I resign myself up unto Thy Holy Spirit, O my God, and my Savior, that He may possess me, and furnish me, and quicken me for Thy service; and carry me through all that I may be called unto. And since all opportunities to serve Thy Kingdom in the world are entirely at Thy dispose, I rely upon Thy providence to find out opportunities for my doing of good; resolving with

Thy help, to be satisfied with what I shall see the thing appointed for me.

Being brought under such a consecration to God, now proceed in your preparation for the service of the Sanctuary. In which, as you pass along, I cannot but wish that the admirable Witsius' oration, *De Vero Theologo*, might be so considerately read by you, as to leave a deep impression upon you.

It is a speech of Jacob Alting with which I am willing your mind should be deeply tinctured; *Majus est in Ecclesia aliquid dixisse, quod ad ejus Edificationim pertineat, quam summa inter Homines Gloria, et Potestate gavisum fuisse.*[1] And I will hereupon mind you of it, that one of the greatest personages (an Archbishop and a Lord-keeper) in the English nation once uttered this memorable speech:

> I have passed through many places of honor and trust, both in church and state, more than any of my order in England, for seventy years before. But were I assured that by my preaching I had converted but one soul unto God, I should herein take more comfort than in all the honors and offices that have ever been bestowed upon me.

You are entering upon a work that will keep you continually in the way of this incomparable satisfaction; and I hope that you will rejoice in the way of bearing testimonies for God more than in all riches; and that the saving, or enlightening and edifying of one soul at any time will be a matter of more joy unto you

---

[1] Translation: "It is a greater thing to have said something in the Church which pertains to its edification than the highest glory among men, and to have rejoiced in the Power."

than if all the wealth of Ophir should flow in upon you. If such men of quality, as George the Prince of Anhalt, and the Lord of Chandieu who goes under the Hebrew name of Sadeel, and the noble John Alasco (to say nothing of Titus, to whom they assign a noble extraction among the Cretans), counted themselves gloriously enriched in opportunities to preach the unsearchable riches of Christ; yea, or if the most opulent monarch that ever Israel had, even Solomon in all his glory, has assumed the title of "The Preacher;" it was no diminution unto their quality to be employed in a work of this importance. I will not say you are taken in among the great men of Achaia, but more than so, God raises the poor out of the dust, and sets you with the princes of His people when He thus employs you. It pleases me when I read such a passage as this drop from the pen of a person of quality in his view of the soul:

> It is certainly the highest dignity, if not the greatest happiness, that human nature is capable of, here in this vale below, to have the soul so far enlightened as to become the mirror, or conduit, or conveyer of God's truth to others.

But then, be armed! Be armed as a good soldier of Jesus Christ for an employment, wherein grievous discouragements, heavy difficulties, more than can be numbered, are to be looked for; and things to be endured, whereof 'tis well for you that you may say, I know not the things that shall befall me!

Be armed for a warfare, wherein you will have wonderful temptations assaulting of you, repeated on you. I need not quote an Ecclesiasticus to tell you so. What low, and mean, and straight circumstances for this world must you probably be confined unto? What mischiefs from the ungodly and unrighteous men that fill this world, will your appearances for the cause of God probably bring upon you? In short, you will find yourself entered into a winepress; and I must give you Austin's advice, *Prepara te ad Pressuras:*[2] But let every one of your pressures fetch good liquor from you. Yea, I will forewarn you of it, that if you move at all out of the common road with singular activities, I believe, you will hardly ever be engaged in any special service for the Kingdom of God, but you shall either just before it, or after it, meet with some special trouble; either in some shock upon your health; or in some storm of groundless and senseless obloquies among the people; or (which is often, the worst of all) some horrid colaphisations from the wicked spirits on your mind, strangely filling you with consternations and confusions, which be they never so unreasonable, yet will be intolerable. There may be some special revenue of Satan in these molestations upon you, for the special service to Christ, at which he is enraged; but there is the wisdom of our faithful Redeemer for holy ends permitting and ordering of them; especially to keep you in the dust, and in the midst of continual annihilations, that the strength of your Glorious Lord, may be conspicuous in the weakness which you find yourself reduced unto. But now, in the foresight of all this, can you bravely resolve:

> O my Savior, though I foresee that I shall be exposed unto many things as uneasy as many deaths, if I go on to lay myself out for the service of Thy Kingdom, yet with Thy help, I will go on; I will do it unto the uttermost. And I will cheerfully rely upon Thee to make

---

[2] Translation: "Prepare yourself for pressures."

me a conqueror, and more than a conqueror, over all. I believe, and I am sure that the issue will be glorious!

My son, the spirit of martyrdom is upon you. You shall be crowned among the martyrs of the Lord.

14
THE MANNER OF READING THE SCRIPTURES

Can a man be a thorough divine without reading the Sacred Scriptures? No, verily; not so much as a common Christian. Read them, child; I say, read them with an uncommon assiduity. To dig in these rich mines, make it your daily exercise. Hold on doing so until you are, I will not say, *Bonus Textuarius*, but until you are an eloquent man and mighty in the Scriptures.

To this purpose, my advice to you is that it be your practice to read the Sacred Scriptures in the porismatic way; or, with a labor to observe and educe the doctrines of godliness, which this inexhaustible storehouse of truth will yield unto them that are seeking after it. Make a pause upon every verse, and see what lessons of piety are to be learned from every clause. Turn the lessons into prayers and send up the prayers unto the God, who is now teaching of you. As arrows from the hand of a mighty man, send them up with lively ejaculations unto the heavens. What exercise can be more enlightening, more sanctifying, more comfortable, than such an intercourse of God uttering His voice, and, lo, a mighty voice!—unto you, and your holy returning of it unto Him in such echoes of devotion! I will say this for your encouragement: in your searching of the Scriptures, you will forever have something that is new to entertain you. They are a treasury which (beyond that at

Venice) you cannot reach to the bottom of. Austin,[1] in his Epistle to Valusius, has not said a thousandth part of what may be said about fetching still every day fresh entertainments and advantages from them, after one has already spent an age in the study of them. The Jews have reason on their side when they say of the Scripture, *Versa eam, et Versa eam, nam onmia sunt in ea.*[2]

I will refine yet a little further upon this proposal; and I will show you an excellent way, how in reading of the Sacred Scriptures, you may make an admirable and effectual application of the leaves, which are for the healing of the nations; and have the inestimable blessings of a healed soul conveyed unto you. What I intend is my Speners direction: *Praemissis Plis Precibus, Affectum Scriptorum Sacrorum Devota Attentione observent, eumque Affectum assumere studeant.*[3] The holy men of God who wrote this astonishing book were moved by His Holy Spirit, in it and for it; and the Spirit of holiness at the time of the inspiration made suitable impressions on the affections of His faithful servants. When the Holy Spirit, with His afflations, disposed them to write what we have in our hands, He doubtless produced in their hearts those motions of piety which were agreeable and answerable to the matter then flowing from their pens. They are very legible, and an ordinary capacity may discover them these motions of piety in the soul; by these things men live, and in all these things is the life of your spirit.

---

[1] Augustine.

[2] Translation: "Engage in it, and engage in it, for all things are in it."

[3] Translation: "Having started with pious prayers, let them cultivate a love for the sacred scriptures with devoted attention, and let them be eager to take up that love."

Reading the Scriptures

Now, do you lay one sentence, and then another, and so a third, of your Bible before you? Find out which of these affections is obvious and evident in the sentence under consideration. Try, strive, do your best, that the same affections may stir, yea, flame in your soul. Be restless till you find your soul harmonizing and symphonizing with what the Holy Spirit of God raised in His Amanuensis at the time of His writing. Be not at rest until you find your heart-strings quaver at the touch upon the heart of the Writer, as being brought into an unison with it, and the two souls go up in a flame together. Consider what affections of piety are plainly discernible in the Word that is before you; and then, with a soul turning unto the Lord, assay to utter the language of the like affections. E're you are aware, you will be caught up to Paradise; you will mount up as with the wings of eagles! I have had opportunity elsewhere to say,

> If I constantly affirm this, that all the Commentators in the world are poor things to interpret the Bible in comparison of an illiterate Christian thus coming with a sanctified soul to make his practical commentary; I could quote a very great person, who will not leave me alone, but will affirm, *Commentarius sine hoc Adminiculo (pio Sacrorum Motuum scrutinio) Conscriptus, est Vere Commentarius, et Nomine, et Omine talis, id est, Commentis cerebri refertus.*[4] Among all the hermeneutic instruments for the opening of the Scriptures, we may say of this: There is none like it.

---

[4] Translation: "Commentary recorded without this aid (the pious scrutiny of divine motivations) is truly such a commentary in both name and sign, that is, filled with fabrications of the brain."

Directions for a Candidate of the Ministry

The commentaries of our [Matthew] Henry on the Bible have out-done most that we have yet had in this regard: the Spirit which dictated the Sacred Scriptures, operating on the mind of the commentator in the dispositions and observations of experimental piety. The erudition also appearing without affectation of appearance in them is far from contemptible. I wish you furnished with them. What is done by [Matthew] Poole and his continuators is highly valuable; and may be of use, not only for occasional inspection, but also for diurnal meditation. How happy should we have been if a Hutcheson who has done so well on Job, and on the smaller Prophets, and on John, had left us the like operations on the rest of the Bible? Or, if a Caryl on Job, a Greenhil on Ezekiel, a Burroughs on Hosea, an Owen on the Hebrews, a Manton on James, and a Jenkins on Jude, were accompanied with others like them on the rest of sacred pandects?

Being upon your daily exercise, I will add no more. But this I would advise you, wherever you in any reading meet with a curious illustration of a text—prize it, seize it, enter it in papers where you may design a lodging for such inestimable jewels. Like Hezekiah, have your treasures for precious stones, and let these be such unto you. Get such an amassment of them that among them you may be like the King of Tyrus; and walk up and down in the midst of the stones of fire when you are upon the holy mountain of God. One of these may be worth an ingot of gold, and a whole discourse may be rendered acceptable by having such a jewel studded in it.

15
Studying a
Body of Divinity

Let the men who corrupt the earth, and have nothing but their cassocks, to claim the name of divines for them. Sit in the seat of the scorner, and laugh, and scoff at all systematical divines as long as they please. There are systems of divinity which I most seriously advise you to be most intimately acquainted with.

And here, either Wollebius' *Manuductio ad Theologiam*, or Amesius' *Medulla Theologiae*, or Marckius' *Compendium Theologiae*; I would have you to get so into your head (and heart!) as to be a perfect master of the system.

Go on then to read, with a strong attention, the *Synopsis Purioris Theologiae* of the Leyden divines. Usher's *Body of Divinity* is orthodox and excellent, and is accommodated with the most agreeable texts of Sacred Scripture upon every article. For this, and all good theological purposes, get as much of and be as much with H. Alting as ever you can. He has been called *Theologus Scripturarius*,[1] and everything of his is valuable. All that is done by that Hund has much of heaven in it. Tuckney's *Prelectiones* are an inestimable treasure. So are those of Prideaux. The works of Hemingius deserve a greater title than

---

[1] Translation: "Theologian of the Scriptures."

that of Opuscula. The *Loci Communes* of Aretius have uncommon riches in them. Edwards' *Theologia Reformata* also will be no contemptible treasure for you on all occasions. You might wonder at me if I should forget Calvin's *Institutes*, to which the concurrent opinion of them that wished well to the Reformed religion assigned a preference before all the writings that the Church of God has enjoyed since the Apostolic; as the well-known Distich has informed you.

Some that have written on *The Creed* are highly worthy of being your instructors. Particularly, a Pearson, and a Witsius. But after all, there is nothing that I can with so much plerophorie recommend unto you as Mastricht's *Theologia Theoretico practica*. That a minister of the gospel may be thoroughly furnished unto every good work, and in one or two quarto volumes enjoy a well-furnished library, I know not that the Sun has ever shone upon an human composure that is equal to it. And I can heartily subscribe unto the commendation which Pontanus in his *Laudatio Funebris* upon the author has given of it: *De hoc Opere confidenter affirmo, quod eo Ordine sit digestum, tanto rerum pondere praegnans et tumidum, tanta et tam varia Eruditione refertum, ut nescio an in illo genere usquam Gentium exstet aliqnid magis accuratum et elaboratum.*[2] I hope you will next unto the Sacred Scripture make a Mastricht the storehouse to which you may resort continually. But above all things, remember the dying words of this true divine, which he uttered *Altissima Voce* (and I wish all that study divinity might hear it!): *Se*

---

[2] Translation: "Concerning this work I confidently affirm, that it may be considered of this rank, that I know of no other anywhere in the world more accurate and elaborate, packed and filled with a great weight of ideas, filled with great and varied erudition."

*nulla Loco et Numero habere Veritatis Defensionem, quam sincera Pietas et Vitae Sanctitas, individuo nexu non comitetur.*³

But if you are laying in for a library, there are two or three divines whose works alone will afford you a copious library, and you may on almost every subject repair unto them, and see what almost every writer has offered upon it. Such more particularly are Gerhard's *Loci Communes*; and Voetius' *Selectae Disputationes, et politia Ecclesiastica*.

Polemical divinity

That you may have a general insight into polemical divinity, and at once make a short visit with safety to the camp in the Valley of Elah, and see the men of Israel fighting with the Philistines, you have much done for you in Prideaux's *Fasciculus*. But there are two little Duodecimo's, which for this purpose are worth more than twelve times their weight in gold; these are the *Turris David* and the *Turris Babel* of the wondrous Alsted. There is also a little book in the English tongue—Sinclare's, *Truth's Victory over Error*—which is worthy to be called *Enchiridion Militis Christiani*.⁴ I will say nothing of a little book published among ourselves under the title of *Supplies from the Tower of David*.

As for more particular controversies in religion, I will not perplex you with a tedious catalogue of what has been best written on the several controverted points. You will not much trouble yourself with them till the providence of God call you to the wars, and bring the occasions for it.

---

³ Translation: "There is no defense of the truth anywhere which sincere piety and the sanctity of life does not accompany in inseparable union."

⁴ Translation: "a handbook for a Christian soldier."

However, that I may leave nothing untouched that you may look for. I will just say thus much: to encounter the Romanists, you will be admirably furnished in the *Panstratia* of a Chamier, or the *Synopsis Papismi* of a Willet, or the very learned works of a Jackson. To confute the Arians, I commend unto you a Waterland, and a Guise, and a Pike. To confute the Socinians, I commend an Owen, an Abbady, and a Cloppenburg, and a Stilling, fleet, and a Bisterfield. Upon the Quinquarticular Controversies, you'll see who's to friend in Prin, his *Antiarminianism*. To which, I would have you add the *Veritas Redux* of an Edwards. The Antipedobaptists have been confuted by such an army of writers, that except I should single out a Baxter, I can scarce tell whom to pitch upon for your assistance. A little conference entitled, *Baptistes*, reprinted among us will give you the sum of the matter. Faldo has done enough against the Quakers. For the "Theologia Gubernetica," as 'tis called, I will only mention to you the *Politia Ecclesiastica* of a Parker; the *Altare Damascenum* of a Didoclavius; the *Fresh Suit* of a Gillespy; a Baxter, of Episcopacy; and a Pierce, his *Vindication of the Dissenters*; and an Owen, *Of the Nature of the Gospel Church*.

But it is of the last importance that you be a good casuist. And an Ames, in his *Casus Conscientiae*, an Alsted, in his *Theologia Casuum*, a Baxter in his *Directory*, and a Baldwin, in his book, *De Casibus Conscientiae*, have done what will abundantly qualify you to pass a judgment upon the cases that may lie before you, and well distinguish the clean from the unclean in your discharge of your ministry.

Abundance has been written to recommend—the study of the Fathers. And it has been recommended by none more than some neotericks and innovators who have had very indirect intentions in it, and hoped that the Fathers might help them with

STUDYING A BODY OF DIVINITY

some traditions, where the Scriptures failed them. What attempts have there been therefore to set the Epistles of Ignatius almost on the level with the Epistles of our inspired Apostles; while after all the learned impertinencies, wherewith some would maintain the larger, and some the lesser copies of those Epistles, and painful disputations on the problem. How many of them are genuine? They are all of them impostures, and not worthy of any notice with you. What ado has there been to set up *The Apostolical Constitutions* as the most valuable part of the New Testament; when they are evidently despicable and detestable forgeries; and the collections of some ignorant Arian in the fifth century? You may be sure that in the study of the Fathers, I shall at least advise you to so much knowledge of them, as Daille in his excellent book, *The Use of the Fathers*, will instruct you in.

But though the Fathers had such errors, that we may most sensibly bless God for His granting us the Scriptures, to be on all accounts better and safer guides unto us, and the Fathers themselves do times without number urge us to take none but the Scriptures for our guides. And their notorious deficiencies in several points of literature laid them under disadvantages enough to pall and spoil our adoration of them! Nevertheless, there are those writings of the Fathers which I would have you no stranger to. If you bestow a perusal upon the Epistles of Clemens Romanus, and the *Apologies* of Justin Martyr, and of Tertullian, and the book of Origen against Celsius, you will do what I would have you to do. And I am willing you should look upon the *Dialogue* of Minutius Faelix as one of the most celebrated monuments of antiquity. But how can I persuade you to peruse all the folio volumes of both the Greek and Latin Fathers? Indeed. I look on Theodoret as the best expositor of the

Directions for a Candidate of the Ministry

Bible among all the Fathers; and there are very notable and refined expositions often occurring in him. Yet I shall direct you to do little more than consult him upon occasion. I value Chrysostom almost as much as much as they tell us Aquinas did, yet I shall only wish you to attend upon him in some select homilies, and consult him upon occasion.

I am not so enamored on Austin, as (like Jansenius) to read over all his *Works* ten times, and his book, *De Gratia*, thirty times; I shall count it enough, if you go through his *Confessions*, and his *Meditations*, and his *De Civitate Dei* (*City of God*), and some numbers of his letters. Scultet, in his *Medulla Theologiae Patrum*, have given you such abstracts of what has been written by many of the Fathers, as your eye to good purpose may dwell upon. But for a more agreeable and profitable study of the Fathers, I shall propose that you go through Dupin's *Ecclesiastical History*; and where you find an account of any subject handled by any Father, which you have a particular inclination to see what they say upon, then turn to the author, and seek for further satisfaction.

16
THE PULPIT & ITS GLORIOUS WORK

After all this preparation for the sanctuary, you are now coming to feed the flocks on the high mountains of Israel; coming into an employment among the people of God, in which, I wish you may prove like the angel in the Revelation that "came down from Heaven and the Earth was lightened with his glory." I am now going to bring you into the pulpit, which I hope you will ascend (as Luther, when he was much older than you, says he still always did!) with a trembling soul; and remembering that you are to stand where that which the Jewish senator said unto the greatest person among them is what the people of God may say unto you: *Non stas coram nobis, sed coram eo qui dixit, Fiat, et factus est Mundus.*[1]

There is a troop of authors, and even a host of God, who have written on the pastoral care from the days of Gregory down to the days of Gilbert; yea, and since these, every year some to this very day. I cannot set you so tedious a task as to read a tenth part of what has been offered on the art, and the gift, and the method of preaching. If you read the *Pastor Evangelicus* of a Bowles; or *The Preacher* of an Edwards; you will do as much this way, as I shall at present ask you to do.

---

[1] Translation: "You do not stand before us, but before him who said, 'Let there be,' and the world was made."

Directions for a Candidate of the Ministry

The first thing which I have to demand of you is that you entertain the people of God with none but well-studied sermons, and employ none but well-beaten oil for the lamps of the golden candlestick. And be nothing like him who was among the Jews called, "The Plagiary Prophet," and whose punishment was not an easy one. Heaven forbid that you should be one of those pitiful parsons to whom there has been that advice given for the discharge of their pastoral care, that they should use other men's sermons rather than make any of their own. But in the choice of these, use great judgment, and not take an author that is too much above themselves; for by that, compared with their ordinary conversation, it will too evidently appear that they are not the authors of their sermons. 'Tis true, the composures of them that have gone before you may be of use unto you, to supply you with useful hints for the composing of your sermons. And some have ingeniously asserted it:

> That a man of mean abilities may come to fall very little short of the ablest preachers, if he so carefully peruse their sermons, as entirely to digest them, and then, laying them out of his view, proceed in his own way, and in his own style, to deliver them.

Let that be as men please; this I insist upon: when you are to preach, you should go directly from your knees in your study to the pulpit. And when you are thus on your knees in your study, you should bewail the faulty defects in your life which the subject you are to treat upon should lead you to a penitent confession of. Humbly bewailing it, also, that your sermon is no better fitted for the awful service that is before you. Your sermon must also be such that you may hope to have the blood of your Savior sprinkled on it, and His good Spirit breathing in

The Pulpit

it. A sermon likewise it must be, that shall discover you to be a workman; and be, like the peace offerings of old, an oblation, which, as the people of God have their share in it, so 'tis presented unto the Glorious God Himself, the Great King, whose Name is venerable. How such things as these can be compatible to stolen sermons, or concomitant with them, I cannot imagine!

I pass on, to advise you, that when you become a settled preacher, the subject of your sermons may be so well chosen, as to do therein the part of a prudent and faithful steward, who dispenses to everyone their food in the season thereof; and a vigilant watchman, contriving such words in season, as will be fitly spoken. You may do well to go through the whole Body of Divinity in a proper method, and therein declare the whole counsel of God. There are also some rich portions and paragraphs of the Sacred Scriptures, wherein the Spirit of God lays together an admirable variety of important subjects, which you may do well to handle in the order wherein He has provided them for you. But still, notwithstanding the connection of your discourses, I would have you leave room for occasional subjects, and have your parentheses of sermons on such things as you may apprehend the necessities of the people may more immediately and importunately call for. So, being as a thick cloud that has water bound up in it, you shall (as the Ancients expounded that passage in Job) distil it in drops, *Juxta Exigentiam Auditorum*.[2]

That you may be led from time to time unto such subjects as may best answer the designs with which your ministry is to be carried on, you must have your eyes ever towards the Lord,

---

[2] Translation: "according to the need of the hearers."

and with solemn supplications look up to Him, who ministers seed to the sower. But let me particularly commend one piece of discretion unto you; which is, that you may be so laid in aforehand, as never to be at a loss, what subject your studies are to proceed upon. From the want of this provision, how often have I known a preacher spend almost as much time in determining what subject he should preach upon, as there need go for the making of a sermon upon it! But I very much object against your being too long upon a subject: which way of tedious amplification must needs leave much of the sacred field unplowed upon, that is too rich to lie always neglected; and produce many sermons as little to the text, as I suspect many of that German divine's were, who undertook to go over the whole book of Isaiah, and was no less than twenty years on the first chapter of it!

And here, I cannot go any further until I have given you my sentiments upon something that calls for a great consideration with you.

The centrality of Christ in preaching

Among all the subjects with which you feed the people of God, I beseech you, let not the true Bread of Life be forgotten; but exhibit as much as you can of a Glorious Christ unto them. Yea, let the motto upon your whole ministry be: *CHRIST IS ALL*. It has been among the grievous things which I have seen in the days of my pilgrimage, that not only in some of the most celebrated sermons which we have seen published on the most illustrious and memorable occasions, a Christ is (not one tenth part so often mentioned, as He is only in the ten first verses of the First Epistle to the Corinthians, I say) not so much as once mentioned, but also some of your great men have it related of them as an instance of their wisdom, that they gave it as their advice unto ministers—that they should not preach much about the Person of Christ. I have thought: would a blessed Paul have uttered such a word?! A Paul, who said, "I determined to know nothing among you, save JESUS CHRIST, and Him crucified" (1 Cor. 2:2).

It is reported by some travelers that, in the Mahometan[3] Mosques, there are sometimes whole sermons on the glories of a Jesus. And shall they who call themselves Christians, and would be honored as ministers of the Christian religion, preach as if they were ashamed of making the glories of Jesus the subject of their sermons; and so rarely introduce Him, as if it were an indecent stoup to speak of Him!? God forbid! I make no doubt of it, that the almost epidemical extinction of true Christianity, or what is little short of it in the nations that profess it, is very much owing to the inexcusable impiety of overlooking a glorious Christ, so much in the empty harangues, which often pass for sermons. Alas, that there should be so many preachers (I can't say of the gospel!) to whom there might be commended as proper for them, the treatise entitled, *Paraenesis ad Pseudo-Evangelicos nostri Saeculi, de CHRISTO DEO ipsis IGNOTO!*[4]

The Holy Spirit of God forever aims at nothing more than what our Savior has declared in that Word: "He will glorify me." And that Holy Spirit withdraws from the ministry which has in it little concern to glorify Him; and it is therefore an unsuccessful ministry. Let your performance in the pulpit be what

---

[3] Muslim.

[4] Translation: "Exhortation to the Pseudo-Evangelicals or our Age, concerning Christ, a God Unknown to them."

Directions for a Candidate of the Ministry

it will, I must freely tell you, *Non sapit mihi, nisi sonuerit ibi JESUS.*[5]

What I wish for and urge to is this: that your knowledge of the mystery of Christ may conspicuously shine in your sermons; and that it may be esteemed by you, as a matchless grace given you, if you may preach the unsearchable riches of Christ unto the world. The heavens do praise that Wonder; the angels in the heavens are swallowed up in the praises of that Wondrous One! Be, like them, never so much in your element as when the Person, the offices, the benefits, the example, the abasement, and advancement of a Glorious Christ are the subjects of your sermons; yea, reckon that the truth is not well discerned, nor the Word of Truth well divided, until you have the truth as it is in Jesus; He is that Light of God in which you will see light, and every truth will be set in its true light before you.

In every article of the treatises which you bring into the assemblies of Zion, ponder upon this: what aspect a Glorious Christ has upon the truth now before you, and let your hearers be made sensible of it. Yea, whatever point you are upon, think: what is there in my Savior which this point leads me to think upon? If you preach on the evil of sin, and the misery of man fallen by sin, still carry your hearers to their mighty and only Savior. When you preach on the duties of a godly, and sober, and righteous life, still carry your hearers to their Savior, as not only affording a pattern for all those things, but also as offering to live, and act, and work in them, as a principle of life, by which alone they can live unto God.

---

[5] Translation: "There is no taste for me" (or "It makes no sense to me") "unless Jesus resounds there." (Bernard of Clairvaux, Sermon 15).

THE PULPIT

Let me tell you, to take the way of Norris and company, to come at the love of God, without a Christ by the Law of the Spirit of Life in us making us free from the Law of sin and of death; verily, 'twill never do! A Mahometan Abubeker in a self-taught philosopher has as high flights of divinity as many of these divines. Be a star to lead men unto their Savior, and stop not until you see them there. Be assured of this: the infinite Son of God is ineffably dear to His Eternal Father; and our Savior has given us this assurance: "If any man serve Me, him will My Father honor" (John 12:26). If you set yourself above all things to glorify the Christ of God, and affect yourself and others with His—how great goodness and beauty! And use all the methods you can devise, that He may be exalted, and be extolled, and be very high; you will be taken in among the favorites of heaven, and be a man greatly beloved. The angels who, with a perpetual veneration and astonishment, stand about His glorious high throne; the ministers who do His pleasure, and are never so well-pleased as when they see Him glorified; these will with delight look upon you as their fellow servant, and will at His orders be on the wing to do marvelous kindnesses for you.

But then, I must here withal advise you, that the genuine *Doctrines of Grace* be all of them always with you as the very salt and soul of your sermons. They will be putrefied things without them! Assert always the necessity of turning and living unto God; and yet such an impotency in the wounded and corrupt faculties of man as renders a supernatural and regenerating work of *Sovereign Grace* necessary for it. Show people how to plead the sacrifice of our Savior, that they may be forgiven, and how to lay hold on His righteousness, that they may be accepted with God. Show people how to overcome, and mortify, and crucify their evil appetites by repairing to the cross of our

Directions for a Candidate of the Ministry

Savior; and how to derive strength from Him for the doing and the bearing of all that they are called unto. Show the people of God how to take the comfort of their *Eternal Election*, and *Special Redemption*, and *Ensured Perseverance*; and at the same time, fetch mighty incentives to holiness from those hopes, which will forever cause those that have them to purify themselves. Gospelize to them all the commandments of the Law, and show them how to obey upon the principles of the Gospel. And how the precepts of the Gospel are also so many promises of it. With a strong application study the *Covenant of Grace*, and let the Spirit of that Covenant animate and regulate all your performances when you bless the Lord in the congregations.

In these truths there are the articles which the church either stands or falls withal. They will be the life of your ministry. Nor can the power of godliness be maintained without them. The loss of these truths will render a ministry insipid and unfruitful; and procure this complaint about the shepherds: "The diseased you have not strengthened, neither have you brought again, that which was driven away."

That you may be well versed in these truths, it will be requisite that your main reading may not be of such books that have been much in vogue, once real and vital piety has been so much banished out of the world, but are as lame in these points, as that which is (unjustly and unsafely enough) entitled, *The Whole Duty of Man*. There is a set of books which of late years have brought in a fashionable divinity; with the authors whereof, I cannot but be in as ill terms, as Gildas was with his British clergy, when with him a man was *Non eximie Christianus*,[6] who did not call them rather the betrayers than the

---

[6] Translation: "not especially Christian."

ministers of the Gospel. I can by no means wish you to take your divinity from them; or to be unacquainted with the castigations which God has raised up one of their church (an Edwards, I mean) to bestow upon them. In short, if a book that pretends to describe the way of a sinner's reconciliation unto God says nothing of, "By the obedience of One, many made righteous" (Rom. 5:19). If a book that pretends to direct a Christian Life says nothing of a conversion to God, and of being joined unto the Lord through His one Spirit quickening of us; and if a book (that shall be written perhaps by one who hath subscribed our Thirty-Nine Articles) dresses up our doctrine of predestination in the fallacious and invidious terms, and the bearskins in which it is now commonly exploded, and proclaims the author did not believe in his heart the Articles and homilies which his prevaricating hand made a subscription to (Or if it be a book that shall anywhere spitefully link Rome and Geneva together): *Hunc tu, studiosc, caveto*.[7] I had as good plainly say, let not Scott and Company be the men of your counsel.

You may expect that I should more positively say what English treatises of practical divinity I would commend unto you. But here I am encumbered, as Hevelius was when he would have so partitioned his accurate *Selenography* as to have done justice unto the names of all the more illustrious astronomers. Yea, so great is the army of them who have published the true Gospel that I cannot pretend unto the long list of them that have come to the help of the Lord. However, there are a few that must be particularized for you.

---

[7] Translation: "Beware this man, O student!"

Directions for a Candidate of the Ministry

More particularly then, if you would see the covenant of God and the Gospel in an Evangelical exhibition of it, let Strong on the *Covenant* (though under the disadvantages of a posthumous work) be precious to you as the golden wedge of Ophir. If you would, see sound doctrine the works of an Owen have it for you. And I am glad to see how much esteemed they are in the North-British Universities. You have a Goodwin that will place you among the children of light, and will give you the very marrow of the doctrine which is according to godliness. He often soars like an eagle; perhaps, you would have been content, if sometimes a little more concisely. Everything of a Polhil is Evangelical and valuable, especially his *Speculum Theologiae in Christo*.

When your heart and your pen want the holy fire to be quickened with you, a Baxter will bring you a coal from the altar for it. Yea, to fetch a metaphor from another element, he may be called, as you may remember who was of old, "An Ocean of Divinity." To say of that very great man, that if he had not meddled in too many things, he would have been esteemed one of the learned men of the age. 'Tis to speak a thing which I don't well understand: for his meddling in so many things, and writing more learnedly upon the most of them (except his Expositions) than the most of them who have written upon perhaps but one or two of the things, to me renders him one of the most learned of the age.

In a Charnock you will have substantial divinity, and of the right sort. A Bates will treat you with angels' food. A Howe will set manly religion before you. In a Flavel, you will find the true savor of plain, lively, useful preaching. What a Collings has written on providence is well performed. And what a Ford has written on *The Spirit of Bondage and Adoption* is as fine as anything I have seen for the experimental. And though a Doolittle may not pass for one of our greatest men, yet having in his book on the Catechism given us the Body of Divinity all in a flame, I am willing that it should be (what Zoroaster called his famous book, *Zundavesta*, which, though written above two hundred and twenty years ago, we still have in our hands), a fire kindler for you; and put you in the way after an awakening manner, to set conscience about its work, when you come to that application with which your sermons are still to be enlivened.

If you go further back, and even up to a Perkins, you will find in many treatises that good old Puritan divinity, which the honors of the old way belong unto: and, no man having drunk that old wine and such books as, the *Christian's Daily Walk* of a Scudder, will much desire the new, but he will say, "The old is better." If we mean to go to heaven, we shall not miss our way by having Isaac Ambrose in our company. I say nothing of a Preston, and a Bolton, and a Capel, and a Fenner, and a Rogers, and a Sibbes, and a Hall—all highly valuable. But I cannot forbear saying, the writings of the Dyke's (both Daniel and Jeremiah) have a singular flavor and vigor in them. Everything of an Arrowsmith is admirable. A Gurnal will furnish you with a magazine of good things. Of an A. Burgess, I may say, he has written for thee excellent things. A Reinolds, too, must be taken into the list of them who have written what none will repent the reading of. His preparations are fat things full marrow; wines from the lees well refined. And some things of a Burroughs, especially his *Moses's Choice*, will not make you complain that you have lost your time in conversing with them.

Directions for a Candidate of the Ministry

In fine: the six volumes of *The Morning Exercises* will give you such a variety, both of matters and of talents that I could wish you may not be without them.

I may not omit giving you the best encouragement I can to allow unto a box of North-British authors a standing in your library, and often resort unto it. The Jews have a fancy that, when our Almighty Creator bespangled the heavens with the stars of light, He left a space near the Northern Pole, unfinished and unfurnished, that if any after-God should lay claim to Deity, a challenge to fill up that space might eternally confute it. But in the firmament of the church, that Northern part which belongs to Scotland, has been illuminated with stars, even enough to make a galaxy.

And though the assiduous employments of the parish and the pulpit, which are enough to take up all the time of their pastors, have prevented (which 'tis a pity!) the appearing of so many writers among them, as might otherwise have dispensed their sweet influences to us; yet their pens have not been idle. Of these we have several commentators on the Sacred Scriptures (among which, a Durham—especially on the commandments! And a Weemse long before him has given us a rich amassment of biblical treasures well worth your having). We have several who have enriched us with bodies of theology (among which, a Scharpius). We have several champions for the *doctrines of grace* (among which, a Rutherford). We have several historians (among which, I will not say, a Spotswood, so much as a Calderwood, and very lately, a Woodrow). We have several defenders of the Gospel-Worship, and the gospel Church-State (among which, a Gelaspy, a Lauder, a Willison, and a Jameson. The eagle-eyed and miraculous man last mentioned, has also obliged us with *Spicilegia Antiquitatum*, which are invaluable and preferable to a whole vintage of many other literators). We have several practical tractators (among which, a Guthry, and a Clark, and that wondrous youth, whose green years could not withhold from him the wisdom and esteem, as he wore the name of Gray!). It had been some injustice as well as ingratitude in me to have left these unmentioned. And if a Burnet might not have been thought a little too much Anglified for it, he should also have had a mention among the illustrious pens of Scotland.

Sermonic Preparation

About the way of studying a sermon, I exhort you, that all be with a spirit of piety, and therefore very prayerfully carried on. 'Tis no more than what the nature and intent of the service highly calls for. First, look up to heaven with dependence upon a Glorious Christ, for His influences and assistances to carry you through what you have in hand. Yea, repeat the invocations with fresh elevations of your eyes to Him from whom comes all your help. Whenever you return after any intermission of your study upon it: "O my God and Savior, without Thee I can do nothing; help me, help me! Send forth Thy light and Thy truth unto me!" This will be equivalent unto the practice of such devout men as a Bradford and a Cartwright, of whom they report, they studied their sermons on their knees.

And when you have dispatched a paragraph of a sermon, I wish it might be a frequent practice with you to make a pause upon it; and get your sermon by heart, I mean, get your heart suitably touched with what you have prepared before you go any further; and cast into the mold of the sanctifying truths by such confessions and such petitions as you may dart up to heaven upon them. At least, let this be done in your perusing of your whole sermon before your preaching of it. Some celebrated preachers have piously declared, they never durst preach a sermon to others till they have got some good by it themselves. To feel what you speak, how wondrously will it qualify you to be a lively speaker! 'Twill bring you to deserve the title of a Rabbi Hadarsan.

Be careful evermore to preach Scripturally, and employ the Sword of the Spirit, if you would hope to do execution. Pertinent Scriptures demonstrating and embellishing every article will well become one who would speak as the Oracles of God. For your aid in this, I cannot but recommend unto your use Ravenellus' *Bibliotheca Sacra*, as one of the most useful books in the world for a preacher, that would at once have in one regular, orderly, advantageous view before him, the sum of what the Scriptures have said on every subject—a work that is moreover full of expositions and illustrations. There is also a book entitled, *A Common Place Book to the Holy Bible*, worth being always at hand with you.

On Using Similitudes (Analogies)

It would be well if you could likewise come to say with the prophet, "I have used similitudes." And accustom yourself to find out similitudes, wherewith you may clothe your ideas, and make them sensible to the lowest and meanest capacities, yea, to all flesh. Thus to seek out acceptable words would render you a most profitable as well as agreeable preacher. It would marvelously fasten the nails, and be some imitation of the preaching which He that spoke so as never man spoke, has given you a pattern for.

In your preaching, that you may save them that hear you, I wish you may with all possible dexterity spread the nets of salvation for them. And therefore often exhibit the terms of salvation, and the proposals of the Gospel, in such a manner, and so importunately soliciting their consent unto them that, by the hearty speaking one word in the echoes of devotion thereupon, they may be brought into them. Exhibit unto them the desires of piety in such a manner that they must have their hearts burn within them, and they must be hearts of stone indeed if they take not fire immediately. When you also describe the graces of the new creature, give the description in the language of piety, acting those graces; wherein, if they come into a consort with you, their souls are gained unto God at the very moment of your instructing them. Oh! That you may be a wise winner of souls! And while you are preaching, may the Holy Spirit fall on them that hear the Word!

On delivery

For this purpose, I would have you usually try, as much as with good judgment you can, to set the truths on fire before you part with any head that you are upon; and let them come flaming out of your hand with excitations to some devotion and affection of godliness, into the hearts of those whom they are addressed unto. The tongues with which the Holy Spirit made His descent on the first and best preachers of the Gospel that ever were in the world were flames and had the appearance of an heavenly fire upon them.

'Tis pity but a well-prepared sermon should be a well-pronounced one. Wherefore, avoid forever all *Inanes sine Mente Sonos*;[8] and all indecencies; everything that is ridiculous. Be

---

[8] Translation: "nonsense sounds without meaning." This exact phrase appears in Brucker's 18th century magnum opus *A Critical*

sure to speak deliberately. Strike the accent always upon that word in the sentence which it properly belongs unto. A tone that shall have no regard unto this is very injudicious; and will make you talk too much in the clouds. Don't begin too high. Ever conclude with vigor. If you must have your notes before you in your preaching, and it be needful for you, *De Scripto dicere*,[9] what even some of the most famous orators both among the Grecians, and among the Romans did (Pliny says, *Orationes, et nostri quidam et Greci Lectitaverunt*[10]), yet let there be with you a distinction between the neat using of notes, and the dull reading of them. Keep up the air and life of speaking, and put not off your hearers with a heavy reading to them. How can you demand of them to remember much of what you bring to them when you remember nothing of it yourself? Besides, by reading all you say, you will so cramp and stunt all ability for speaking, that you'll be unable to make an handsome speech on any occasion. What I therefore advise you to is: let your notes be little other than a quiver on which you may cast your eye now and then to see what arrow is to be next fetched from thence; and then, with your eye as much as may be on them whom you speak to, let it be shot away with a vivacity becoming one in earnest, for to have the truths well entertained with the auditory.

Optimus est Orator, qui dicendo, Animos Audientium, et decet, et delectat, et permovet.[11]

History of Philosophy, a possible allusion to Seneca, *De Beneficiis* 4.27, but more likely a general allusion to 1 Cor. 14:10-11.

[9] Translation: "to speak from what is written."

[10] Translation: "Certain of our speakers and the Greeks read their speeches."

[11] Translation: "He is the best speaker who speaks what is suitable, delightful and moving to the spirits of his audience."

The Pulpit

Finally, let your perorations (from which, *Noscitur Orator*) often be lively expostulations with the conscience of the hearer; appeals made, and questions put unto the conscience, and consignments of the work over into the hands of that flaming preacher in the bosom of the hearer. In such flames you may do wondrously!

17

EMPLOYMENTS FOR A VIGILANT PASTOR

Upon the due discharge of the pastoral duties, in which you must labor to know the state of your flock, and lay hold on all occasions to drop the lessons of piety upon them; and how to manage the pastoral visits with an admirable dexterity and fidelity; and therein to be forever scattering books among them, which may be lasting monitors unto them, and a salt for their preservation; yea, and be scattering alms, like the liberal showers from above upon the indigent among them: I suppose I need now do no more than give a short hint unto you that such things are to be thought upon. All that I will now say to you upon this pastoral watchfulness is this: when certain "shepherds were keeping watch over their flocks, lo, the Angel of the Lord came upon them, and the glory of the Lord shone round about them!"

Catechizing

Among the employments of a vigilant pastor, I cannot avoid saying of something, *De Catechizandis Rudibus*;[1] and putting you in mind that great things may be done in the way of

---

[1] Translation: "about catechizing the young." (*Rudibus* could refer literally to children or to those who have recently become Christians).

catechizing. A work this is for which the greatest men in the church of God have not thought themselves too great. And some eminent persons coming towards a superannuation for other services have, by applying themselves almost wholly to this, continued very serviceable to the last. In this exercise, to break the answer now and then into smaller questions, and so drop it into narrow-mouthed understandings; and thereupon to graft exhortations, which may draw the catechumens into the declared resolutions of piety; and more particularly show them the blessings for which they are to make their supplications, and gain a promise from to do so. This is one of the things where an abundance of wisdom and prudence may be demonstrated.

Among the many hundreds of catechisms which have made their way into the world, what is now most in use is *The Assemblies*, which was composed by Dr. Tuckney, Dr. Arrowsmith, and Mr. Newcomen, and adopted and emitted by the most venerable convention of divines that was ever seen in our nation. But some have thought that this, like all other human composures, might be capable of some amendment. And I could myself particularly wish that among the articles of, the misery of the estate into which man fell, there might be inserted, and enslaved unto the powers of darkness. And that among the articles of, Christ executing the office of a Priest, there might be this clause inserted: "In performing perfect obedience to the Law of God, the everlasting rule of righteousness." And that among the benefits which in this life do accompany justification, there might be inserted, "The ministry of good angels for our good, and succor against the temptations of the devils.

Employments

Though it is not for you to correct the catechism, yet you may, in your catechizing, do justice to these important articles. Up, and be doing; and be thus, an Instructor of the young; yea, an angel to the little ones.

Private prayer

But no good is to be any further expected from you than it may be reported of you, "Behold, he prays!" You must, like the camel, receive all your burdens on your knees. And your whole work must be carried on with a continual praying over it.

For your secret prayers, I can bate you nothing of David's and of Daniel's number, three times in a day. For your pious ejaculations, I have nothing against the number which they report of the Apostle Bartholomew (one hundred in a day!). Yea, or that which they report of a Father whose name was Paulus (three hundred in a day!). If you can attain so far to have your eyes ever towards the Lord. Excellent is the counsel of Lansbergius in his *Enchiridion Militis Christiani*, (And by the way, Erasmus' golden book of the same title, I earnestly advise you to the reading of!): *Ex Omnibus quae vides, quaequae audis, disce orandi sumere Occasionem, mentemque ad Deum elevandi.*[2]

Besides your stated prayers for every day, you will also have numberless errands to heaven, which will oblige you frequently to make your occasional addresses thither upon emergencies. But what in a very particular manner I advise you to is, now and then, to set a part *whole days* for interviews with heaven; and this with such fasting as you may find you are able to bear, and may be for the help of your devotions. On such

---

[2] Translation: "From everything which you see and hear learn to find an occasion for speaking and elevating the mind to God."

days, go through a process of repentance, which cannot be too often repeated. Renew your flights unto your Savior, that you may be more quickened in the life of God. Present the sacrifices wherein you shall offer up your all unto Him, and embrace and enjoy a Christ instead of all. Carry to Him all your concerns; and let all your desire be before Him, and none of your groaning be hid from Him. Let your petitions for others, and for all the societies you belong unto, express the true spirit of grace in your supplications, and be like those of the man greatly beloved. Soar up as high as you can towards a union with God. Intermix all along the reading of proper things, wherein God from the Holy Oracle may commune with you; and you may assist and inflame the work wherein you are engaged. Let the minutes of spaces between your devotions be filled with reflections that may tend to bring you into abasements of yourself, or into adorations of your God; and from your heart within you, let them go up silently unto the Lord. Conclude all with holy projections and purposes for further improvements in a careful, fruitful, humble walk with God.

But how much could I wish that in this religion of the closet, you may know what it is to keep days of thanksgiving too? Such days you may fill with contemplations on the perfections of the Infinite God, and the glories of your Almighty Redeemer, and the wondrous things which He has done; and the ministry of His angels. And with enumerations of the favors, which both on spiritual and on temporal accounts you have received from Him; whereof you should make explicit acknowledgements unto your powerful and merciful benefactor, and particularly see and own how undeserved they have been, and how distinguishing they have been, and how the contrary sufferings of Christ have purchased them.

You will upon trial find a day of the Summer Solstice too short for the pleasant work now before you. Here you may intermix the songs of the redeemed; adding the perusal of what you may find written for the help of the heavenward salleys, wherein you are mounting up as with the wings of eagles. You will do well to keep the holy fire alive all the day by making all the objects which occur to you in the intervals of your devotions but a fuel that your praises to God shall seize upon, and go up in short motions of soul unto Him.

Conclude all with an ingenuous meditation on that question: what shall I render to the Lord for all His benefits? These days will not only obtain marvelous blessings for you, but also leave a celestial flavor and grandeur on your mind, and infuse a becoming discretion and gravity into all your conversation.

A word on prayer in general

One consequent of these things will be; what I am very solicitous you should arrive unto, that is to say, an ability to express yourself in prayer to the Glorious God, and spread the cases of the people before Him on all occasions—an ability without which I shall not judge you qualified for an ordination to the pastoral care of a flock among the churches of God; but worthy to have an *ANAXIOS* cried out upon you.

In your doing this, you will have notable opportunities to bring them into the frames of piety, which are to be wished for them.

Whatever truths at any time you would most efficaciously preach unto them, you may make them hear you pray down these truths into them with a most surprising and most subduing efficacy.

Directions for a Candidate of the Ministry

I can by no means approve of your leaning on the tool of a foolish shepherd, and your living on the lifeless forms of any liturgy. I cannot commend any liturgy to you except that which Baronius taxed good old Agobardus for keeping to. I can do no other than tell you so, after a Bellarmine himself has confessed,

> That in old times, there was no form of prayer prescribed, for all to be bound unto, but every one might make what prayer he pleased, if but the Analogy of Faith were kept unto.

And Chemnitius, with a whole army of Protestants, have irrefragably proved that this confession of Bellarmine is true; and, *Apud Veteres Ordinem Celebrandi fuisse Arbitrarium.*[3] The Ancients all agree to it that, in the earlier days of Christianity, the ministers prayed everywhere as they were able. Indeed, there was no general imposition of any service book until the Emperor Charlemagne at the solicitation of the Pope introduced it with persecution; which was not until the entrance of the ninth century when all manner of superstitious usages were brought into the temple of God. Some judicious men have complained of the French liturgy composed by the excellent Calvin for not having sufficient collects of thanksgiving, but being all petition. And whereas these three things—confession, and petition, and thanksgiving—belong to every complete prayer. I have heard some enquire whether according to this rule, there can be readily found one complete prayer in another liturgy which I cannot commend unto you for such a model of perfection, as its admirers have esteemed it. But waving here those

---

[3] Translation: "Among the ancients there was no set order for worship."

many and weighty exceptions against the English Common Prayer-Book, which will forever cause myriads of considerate Christians to be dissatisfied with it, I will only quote some words that I find falling from the pen of an English nobleman.

> There may be too great a restraint, [he says] put upon men, whom God hath distinguished by giving them not only good sense, but a powerful utterance too. When a man so qualified, endued with learning too, and above all, adorned with a good life, breaks out into a warm and well-delivered prayer before his sermon, it has the appearance of a divine rapture. He raises and leads the hearts of the assembly in another manner, than the most composed or best studied form of set words can ever do. And the *Pray Wee's*, who serve up all their sermons with the same garnishing, would look like so many statues, or men of straw in the pulpit, compared with those who speak with such a powerful zeal that men are tempted at the moment to believe that heaven itself has dictated these words unto them.

I cannot but think that good sense was that which dictated these words unto the Marquess of Halifax. And I hope your prayers will be such as he has therein described unto you.

Warning & encouragement
I am sorry that I must (but I must!) conclude my advice for your diligence in the discharge of the pastoral duties with a warning, that you must not wonder at it, if you find that you serve many ungrateful people, and may be many ways maltreated by them who are under the strongest obligations to support you, and reduced unto the humbling and creepling circumstances of a *Res*

Angusta Domi;[4] yea, be oppressed with grievous defraudations from them whom God will many ways punish for their ingratitude.

If it should be so, yet remember, you are in the service of a Glorious Lord who not only says, "I know thy service," but orders those things to fall out upon which He may with infinite pleasure also say, "I know thy patience." Be not now discouraged from still devoting yourself to the public and private labors of your ministry. Be wholly in them, and therein labor to overcome evil with good (Rom. 12:21). Suffer anything rather than in the methods of the law, do that which will ruin the success of the Gospel, and utterly extinguish the hope of your doing any more good by your ministry among them. Cause them to feel that you are travailing with agony for the eternal salvation of them and theirs; and that the gaining of one soul to God by your ministry will be of more account with you than any gain of this world than all the wealth in the world.

Be they never so unjust, yet nobly hold on raining the blessed showers of heaven upon them! Thus with a strong faith which gives glory to God, go on with a watchful, painful, faithful ministry; keeping your eye on the sixth chapter of Matthew, and relying on your Savior for your subsistence. And, *Never fear! Never fear!* He will, with strange interpositions of His providence, yea, with conspicuous and marvelous operations of the angelical ministry, send in seasonable supplies for you; and often make the season of them such as notably to add unto the comfort of them.

---

[4] Translation: "restraints of poverty," "limited means."

Yea, sooner than starve, the ravens will bring food unto you. Regenvolscius relates it in his, *History of the Sclavonic Churches*:

> It was a wretched custom of the Papists that when they had run one of the holy people into prison, they would there, by a progressive subtraction of all subsistence from him, starve him to death. Matthias Dolanscius was a prisoner designed for such circumstances, in the city of Prague—and at length all the attempts of the godly people, and of a gracious matron among the rest, secretly to relieve him, had a total stop given to them. Now, one day, when he was on the very point of starving, he cast his eye towards the grate of the prison, and saw a little bird sitting there with something in his bill. His curiosity leading him thither, the bird flew away, but left a bit of cloth, in which, when he took it up, he found a piece of gold. And with this piece of gold, he found ways tolerably to furnish himself with bread until the death of the King, on and by which he obtained his full deliverance.

This I will say to you: *Hold on, Hold on*—always at work for a Glorious Christ; and rather than you should starve, Matthias Dolanscius's bird shall be sent unto you! And unto that question, lacked you anything? You shall be able to give a comfortable answer.

18
THE GENUINE TEMPERAMENT OF A MINISTER

Too weighty are the words of the pious Hen. Will. Ludolf[1] to be left untranscribed, when I am treating you with the things which I am desirous to have greatly considered with you.

> It a great unhappiness that the greatest part of the clergy of all communions do not perceive that God is upon His way to break down all the false draughts and schemes, which the Antichristian spirit of sectarianism hath contrived instead of substantial Christianity, which is, *The restoring of the image of God in the new creature, or the Kingdom and Life of God within us.*

I press you to employ the deepest meditation on this important matter. When the Lord God Omnipotent comes to shake not the earth only, but also Heaven, it is that those things that cannot be shaken may remain. What are those things that cannot be shaken? But those MAXIMS of the *Everlasting Gospel*, wherein all good and wise men are united, and all men become good and wise when they come into that union with them. The MAXIMS, which the more they are studied, and the wiser and the better they are who study them, the more they will be approved of. The MAXIMS which are directly calculated for the grand intentions of, "Glory to God in the highest, and peace

---

[1] Heinrich Wilhelm Ludolf (1655–1710).

on earth from a good will in men towards one another." 'Tis even the first born of my wishes for you that you may be one of those angels that shall fly through the midst of heaven with this Everlasting Gospel, to preach it unto them who dwell on the earth, and move all the people of God, though of different persuasions in lesser points, to embrace one another upon the generous maxims of it, and keep lesser points in a due subordination unto the superior maxims, and manage their differences upon those lesser points with another spirit than what the disputers of this world in the several sects of Christians keep commonly cutting one another withal.

To assist you in the discovering and determining of these everlasting MAXIMS, I will not merely refer you to the sentiments of a judicious Davenant in his *Adhortatio ad Fraternam Communionem inter Evangelicas Ecclesias*, or those of a sharp-sighted Baxter, who was a pen in the hand of God when he wrote his *Catholic Unity*, and *The True and Only Way of Concord*. Much less will I prosecute the proposal of our celebrated Usher:

> That if at this day we take a survey of the several professions of Christianity that have any large spread in any part of the world, and should put by the points wherein they differ from one another, and gather into one body the rest of the Articles wherein they all generally agree; we should find that, in those propositions which without controversy are so universally received in the whole Christian world, so much truth is contained, as being joined with holy obedience, may be sufficient to bring a man unto everlasting salvation. Neither have we cause to doubt, but that as many as do walk according to this rule, (neither overthrowing that which they have built by superinducing

any damnable heresies thereupon, nor otherwise vitiating their holy faith with a lewd and wicked conversation). Peace shall be upon them.

I will rather exhibit the MAXIMS in such a manner as to make the best provision against that loathsome thing, *A Lifeless Religion*; whereof an irreligious life will be the natural consequence. In short, I may as with a burning glass (Oh! That with an irresistible heat from heaven upon you!), contract into a little room, the sum of the matter, and the piety which will be sound a sure foundation for a union among all parties of true Christians, however they may be denominated or distinguished. As our Savior, whom His Father hears always, has prayed for His people that they all may be one, so it is impossible that all the genuine people of God should not unite with one another in much greater things than those in which it is possible for them to dissent from one another. Such things are those *Graviore Evangelii*, which to cut short the work in righteousness, I shall in these three MAXIMS compendiously set before you:

I. The One Most High God, who is the Father, and the Son, and the Holy Spirit, must be my God. And I must make it the main intention of my life to serve and please Him in all holy obedience and submission to Him, remembering that His eye is always upon me; and be afraid of everything which His light in my soul shall condemn as an evil thing.

II. A Glorious Christ, who is the eternal Son of God, incarnate and enthroned in the Blessed Jesus, is the Redeemer on whose great sacrifice I must rely for my reconciliation to God, looking to Him, at the same time, that I may live unto God by Him. Living in me; and under His conduct I am now to expect a blessedness in a future state for my immortal soul; to which He will restore my body when He shall come to judge the world.

III. Out of respect unto God and His Christ, I must heartily love my neighbor, and forever do unto other men as I must own it reasonable for them to do unto myself.

The foundation of God is in these Holy Mountains. While these glorious MAXIMS are (as why should they not be? I am sure much more questionable ones are daily required for to be) subscribed unto, it is to be wished that these two (I can scarce call them—two more) may in subserviency to the first three, be also brought into the subscription.

IV. I adhere to the Sacred Scriptures as the sufficient rule, for belief, and worship, and manners among the people of God, and I would maintain a brotherly fellowship with all good men in the things wherein I apprehend them to follow these divine directions.

V. I declare for the just liberties of mankind and of our nations: and for a Christian encouragement in the church for all that observe the grand MAXIMS of PIETY, accompanied with a free indulgence of civil rights in the state, unto all that approve themselves faithful subjects and honest neighbors, and such inoffensive livers, that human society cannot complain of disturbance from them.

I will not now suppose a quinquarticular controversy, but rather propose a ternarticular period of all controversies. And the very first thing that I offer upon it is that, in these MAXIMS of godliness, which are all without controversy, you behold all controversies of religion as coming to an amicable and a

Genuine Temperament

comfortable period. My advice to you is: when you make some figure in the field of the church-militant, you be drawn as little as may be into any eristic writings; wherein you shall be surprised unawares into the errors of passion, and into the follies of taking pains to convince a few readers that you have more wit than your antagonist. Every man who pulls at the polemic saw, and manages any controversy in religion, always pretends a zeal to uphold in the issue of the disputation some certain point of practical PIETY, which is in these indisputable MAXIMS declared for. If it were not from a zealous concern which the contenders have that the practice of piety may not suffer in such a point, they profess that they would not contend so earnestly for the faith. If they can't sincerely make this profession, they are but litigious, and vexatious, and the gladiators are to be hissed off the theatre by all that wish well to Christianity.

Now, how commonly arc both parties well agreed in the point of PIETY, which the one says he can't be preserved but upon his positions; and the other says he can't be preserved if his be denied? Be sure, all the truly pious are so! But if both parties are agreed for that PIETY which is the main and the scope of all, how much good may you do if you can so syringe the odoriferous water of the confessed MAXIMS upon them, that the quarrelling hives in the loss of their distinction may give over their quarrels, and the children of Jacob not fall out by the way, or be so angry about the way, seeing they are brethren? Or, if the brethren will yet fall out, and the controversies must go on, and you are called forth to bear a part in them, yet, my son, continue to play these engines for the extinguishing of the fires; govern your mind, and your pen, by the MAXIMS of

Directions for a Candidate of the Ministry

PIETY; persuade others what you can to do so too; and carry not on any but the wars of the Lamb in your contestations.

What I could most of all wish for is that for your defense of the truth, which is always for PIETY, you do what you have to do, mostly in that positive way of asserting, and evincing, and advancing the PIETY, which the truth you would have to be defended, is to animate. Conscience will quickly come in with a testimony on the behalf of that PIETY; and the truth which appears necessary to support that PIETY will easily be taken in, and not easily parted with. This is for the most part better than the elenctic way of sheltering the truth from the assaults which they that corrupt the earth would make upon it. Instead of swords, it is to employ plough-shares. Instead of spears, it is to employ pruning-hooks. And the state and work of Paradise is a little emulated and anticipated.

But, if the elenctic way become necessary to be taken, and if you must go down into the Battel and smite the enemies in the Valley of Salt, I again, and again say, take heed unto your spirit. Let the designs of PIETY regulate your whole proceeding. Furnish no new matter for the old complaint of—*Sibi ferales plerique Christiani*;[2] and add nothing to the instances of such outrages as the Jesuits have with derision censured in the controversial writings of the mutual firings between the Lutherans and the Calvinists.

Lutherans and Calvinists! Inasmuch as I have thus unawares mentioned these, I will upon these make the experiment (whether with any better success than my dear Pitiscus did, I know not!), how far a syncretism of PIETY will unite the people of God, or abate their cursed anger and cruel wrath against

---

[2] Translation: "Most Christians are dead in themselves."

one another in pursuing of religious controversies. The sagacious Baron Pussendorf, while he despairs not of breaking down the partition wall between those two mighty parties of Protestants, in other parts of it, yet it appears unto him little short of desperate when the sublime and obscure doctrines of predestination (wherein Luther and Calvin themselves were better agreed than their followers) come to be considered. However, even here also at last he takes courage and says, "If ever there is to be a better condition of mankind, and a happier state of the world, it is not to be expected, but from a serious and universal practice of Christian PIETY." Let us then with a little patience hear both parties declare themselves.

Say, Master Lutheran, what is the PIETY for the maintaining whereof you so eagerly advance your principles? His answer is:

> I would not have the most holy and sin-hating Lord, reproached as the impeller of the sin whereof He is the Revenger. I would not have our Merciful Father blasphemed, as dealing after an illusory manner with men, when He invites them to His Mercy. I would not have any among the fallen race of the First Adam, shut out from the just hopes of life in the death of the Second Adam. I would not have impenitent unbeliever cast upon God the blame of their impenitency; but the wicked lay wholly on themselves the fault of their own destruction. I would have men work about their own salvation with a much diligence and vigilance, as if all turned upon their own will and care whether they shall be saved or no.

The pious Calvinist hears all this with pleasure, and can say, "My brother, in all these things my heart is with you."

Directions for a Candidate of the Ministry

But now, Master Calvinist, it is your turn. Say, what is the PIETY for the maintaining whereof you so eagerly prefer your principles? His answer is:

> I would have our good God forever adored as the Original of all the good that we have or that we do. If men arrive to any good spiritual as well as temporal, I would have our God praised for it; and I would have His favors confessed as most unmerited by us in all our praises. I would not admit the least insinuation, as if the King Eternal, who is the only wise God, had not an infallible foreknowledge from all eternity of whatever comes to pass in time. I would have all that come unto everlasting life, to admire the everlasting love of God unto them; and with endless admirations own that their Savior has done more for them than for others. I would have men look up to God with ardent prayers for His gracious, and enlightening, and sanctifying influences, and pray unto Him as the God of all grace, and the God who gives repentance, and remember that faith is the gift of God. I would have man to be very humble, and humbly to annihilate himself before the Glorious God with Whom there is terrible majesty.

The pious Lutheran hears all this with delight, and can say, "My brother, my heart cannot but concur with you in such things as these."

At the same time, they both find that the several schemes with which they would have this PIETY served are encumbered with insuperable difficulties; and the Lutheran may have retorted upon him those very difficulties which he thinks he sees the Calvinist overwhelmed withal. The old law, *Qui non*

Genuine Temperament

vetat cum potest Jubet,[3] encumbers Arminius with as hard consequences as he charges on Gomarus. Maimonides will tell you how much the Jewish world, and Cicero how much the pagan, has been divided in their opinions, *De Fato* (indeed). Among the Papists, how do the Dominicans, and after these, the Jansenists, and their opposites, keep in the dark, buffeting one another upon them? So that after all, 'tis PIETY that must bring all to rights; and Melancthon's resolution: *Officium agamus, et Disputationes de Predestinatione seponamus.*[4]

The experiment may be made on many other doctrines (among which, I pray, take notice, you'll never find me mentioning the damnable heresies of the Arian and the Socinian!), wherein they that have the true fear of God, and love of Christ, may have their differing sentiments—*Incolumi semper Amicitia.*[5]

Instead of my going on to do that, I rather pass now to say that I would have you lay aside all thoughts of any foundation for a union among the professors of Christianity, but what shall be in the unity of the Spirit; or that work of the Holy Spirit on the hearts of men that inclines them to glorify God with an obedience to His will revealed in His Word, and glorify Christ with a dependence on Him for all their happiness; and love their neighbor as themselves. Other foundation can no man lay! All attempts to build the Tower of Zion on any other foundation

---

[3] Translation: "He who does not forbid when he may commands." Seneca, *Troades* 291 (Mather gives a shortened version of the original, *qui non vetat **peccare**, cum possit, iubet*, "he who does not forbid **sin** when he may commands it").

[4] Translation: "Let us pursue our office, and lay aside disputes about predestination."

[5] Translation: "Always in sound friendship."

will come to nothing; you'll prosper no better in them than they who go to build a Tower of Babel.

But then, let *all* that are by visible PIETY qualified for it find a due and a kind reception with you. Let your feet stand in a large place, and "add unto your faith, godliness, and unto your godliness, brotherly-kindness, and unto your brotherly-kindness, charity" (2 Pet. 1:7). And pay the regards of brethren in Christ, unto all those who, by owning and living the everlasting MAXIMS of PIETY, may claim what the true citizen of Zion will yield unto them that fear the Lord. Allow to, yea, challenge for this people, the rights which belong unto them, and the liberties with which the Son of God has made them free. The people who worship God in the Spirit, and who rejoice in Christ Jesus, and who have no confidence in the flesh, or value not themselves upon a religion which is nothing but flesh and exterior; these are the true people of God—the people which have the promises in the covenant of God pertaining to them; and whereto the kindnesses or the injuries that are done are done unto their Glorious Head in the Heavens. Be not such a Donatist as to dream that the people of God are nowhere to be found but in one party, which you have your greatest esteem for. But, look for them, as to be found under various forms; and let your judgment, how it fares well or ill with the people of God in the world, fetch its measures not from the good or bad circumstances of one party only, but from the prevailing or the suppressing of true PIETY, and what has a tendency to that, wherever it is to be met withal.

Challenge for this people: a power to associate, or form assemblies for the worship of God our Savior according to the directions which they apprehend His Gospel has given them.

Genuine Temperament

Challenge for the societies of this people: the power to elect their own pastors, which was one of the last things lost in the robberies which the Man of Sin committed on the Temple of God.

Challenge for these particular churches: the rights of sacred corporations that have all the needful power of self-preservation and self-reformation; yet obliged in things of common concern, so far to act in conjunction with other churches walking in the faith and order of the Gospel, as to consult them and be directed and restrained by them on just occasions.

For communion in these churches and admission to all the privileges and advantages of the Evangelical Church-State, I would have you insist upon it that no terms be imposed but such necessary things as heaven will require of all who shall ascend into the Hill of the Lord, and stand in His holy place. Be sure to stand by that golden rule, "Receive ye one another, as Christ has received us unto the glory of God;" that is to say, those of whom it is our duty to judge, that our Savior will receive them to His glory in the heavenly world, we ought now to receive unto all the enjoyments of our Christian fellowship. And let the Table of the Lord have no rails about it that shall hinder a godly Independent, and Presbyterian, and Episcopalian, and Antipaedobaptist, and Lutheran, from sitting down together there.[6] Corinthian brass would not be so bright a composition as the people of God in such a coalition, feasting together on His holy mountain.

---

[6] Mather was considered progressive in his ecumenism. However, he only advocated such 'ecumenical' fellowship for Gospel-affirming denominations, and utterly rejected Roman Catholicism.

Directions for a Candidate of the Ministry

I wish, they do not see the fate of Corinth to compel them to it! Though in the church that I serve, I have seen the grateful spectacle! This I must say; a church that shall banish the children of God from His holy Table, and shall exclude from its communion those that shall be saved, merely for such things as are consistent with the maxims of piety, does not exhibit the Kingdom of God unto the world, as a church ought to do. Churches that will keep up instruments of separation, which will keep out those that have the evident marks and claims of them that are one with Christ upon them are, in reality, but combinations of men who, under pretense of religion, are pursuing some carnal interests. Their Diana is very visible!

'Tis a complicated profanity and hypocrisy that these churches are to stand indicted for. It is to be lamented that more churches than one have the guilt of a very sinful schism to be charged upon them for their chasing from their communion, and the annexed encouragements and emoluments, many of the Righteous Nation, which have the gates of heaven standing open for them. And yet such is the mystery of iniquity that, at the same time, they make outcries of schism against the conscientious people for keeping out, while they violently shut the doors upon them. Yea, there has been one church (Tho' I have never heard of but one!) which has punished and even destroyed multitudes of godly men for not conforming to things which the imposers themselves have confessed indifferent.

I hope I have said enough to disengage you from all schismatical combinations and intimate the catholic spirit, which I would have to be exercised in the whole progress of your ministry. *Catholicism without Popery* is the title of an essay which therefore I particularly commend unto a perusal with you.

Genuine Temperament

Finally, as it must be the grand aim of your ministry to propagate the PIETY of the Everlasting Gospel; and though vain men may boast what they will of this or that being the best-constituted church in the world, and celebrate their own admirable constitution, yet that should be esteemed by you the best constituted church in which the piety of the grand Evangelical maxims is most animated and exhibited; and that the best constitution which is most calculated for the cultivation of this indisputable PIETY. So, I would have you go forth to it under a strong tincture of this apprehension: that a church which makes the terms of communion very different from the terms of salvation, and excludes from any means of salvation or from any due expressions of brotherly-kindness, those whom it is a duty to acknowledge as brethren in Christ, is guilty of an iniquity against which all good men ought to hear a testimony.

There are concurring with you hundreds of thousands of generous minds, in which this apprehension lies now shut up as an *Aurum Fulminans*.[7] But it will break forth more and more as the Day approaches, and as men improve in manly religion, in explosions that will carry all before it. And the mean, little, narrow souls that know no religion but that of a party, and their secular interest, will become deserted objects for the disdain and pity of them who have taken the way that is above them. I hope you will do all you can to strengthen your brethren, as God shall give you (And may He give you!) opportunities.

To have done: my concern to see you a *divine of the right stamp* will not permit me to conclude without one little piece of over-weight added unto the advice that has been given you.

---

[7] Translation: "Explosive powder" apparently made from gold (aurum), and quite volatile. Today we might "nitroglycerin."

Having established yourself in sound theology by reading such systems as I have already told you of; unto which, I cannot but now tell you an admirable Turretin should be annexed, as one hardly to be equaled; nor is Cocceius de Faedere to be omitted: (If I said nothing of P. Martyr, and of Polanus, and of Musculus, and of Bucanus, and of Ursinus, and of Essenius, and of the *Theses Salmurienses*, and several more, it was not because I despised them, nor would I have you to do so. However I allow you to make that interpretation of my silence about those they call "The School-Men"—among whom, if you have the sum of Aquinas, you have the sum of all that I shall commend unto you).

Now bestow some reading on a few books, which refer to the Christian Ascetics; and which teach the *Orthodox Pietism*; and which are designed peculiarly to kindle and cherish the Life of God in the soul of man. Read particularly Thomas a Kempis' *De Imitatione Christi*; Gerhard's *Meditationes*; Besoldus' *Axiomata Philosophiae Christianae*; Spener's, *De Natura & Gratia*; and Voetius' *DeExercitijs Pietatis*. I stop here, as I have done heretofore, for that reason, *Discentem Onerat Librorum Turba, non Instruit.*[8] I wish that you may feel good impressions from these, and that what has been called the *Apotheosis Christiana*, may be what you shall thus arrive unto.

---

[8] Translation: "The throng of books burdens the one learning, but does not equip him."

19
RULES OF HEALTH

I have yet more to do. I may not leave you until I leave a few *rules of health* with you; which I shall do with the utmost brevity.

Having first encouraged you to cultivate an intimate acquaintance with some wise and good physician, who may have the continual inspection of your health in your friendly conversation with him, I will defend you with the ensuing admonitions.

I. The most acute physicians find themselves compelled, with our Cheyne, unto this general direction. The grand secret and sole method for long life, and so for the health which will befriend and sweeten it is to keep the blood and juices in a state of due fluidity. And nothing will do this but keeping much to a spare, lean, fluid sort of a diet. All who live long, and without much pain, and after such a life at length die easily, are such as live abstemiously.

II. Borellus has a remark on many students falling into a consumption that it often proceeds, *A Fumo candelarum hausto in Musaeis undi {que} Clausis.*[1] You will undergo the less of this hazard if you mind the report of Manlius: *Ego multos Periculosos*

---

[1] Translation: "From the draught of candle smoke always contained in the halls of learning."

Directions for a Candidate of the Ministry

Morbos et Miserias hujus Corpusculi mei Vito, hac unica Ratione, quod semper utor Diligentia, cito eundi cubitum.[2]

III. The *Medicina Gymnastica* has done miraculous things. Bodily exercise profits; but no exercise comparable to that of moderate riding; whereof, the reason why we find no more in the prescriptions of the Ancients, (tho' Galen has a chapter about it) for the recovery of the feeble, is because they were so simple as to ride without stirrups. The saddle is the seat of health. As for the games which exercise the spirit and not the body, particularly the noble and ancient game of Chess, these are by no means proper for a student.

IV. 'Tis an observation of that great man, the Lord Verulam, *Nihil magis conducit ad Sanitatem et Longaevitatem, quam Crebrae et Domesticae Purgationes.*[3] A family-purge now and then taken may be of service to you. Pillulae Ruffi,[4] especially when chalybeated[5] with adding about a third part of Sal Martis;[6] Or else, a bottle of Aniseed water,[7] with a dram or two of rhubarb steeped in it; these you may conveniently have always at hand for this purpose.

V. Vander Heidan has not related a hundredth part of the virtues in cold water. I tender you the advice which the aged servant of God gave to his valued son, "Drink not only water;

---

[2] Translation: "I avoid many dangerous diseases and troubles for this frail body of mine by following one simple rule diligently: go to bed on time." Literally: "quickly going to bed."

[3] Translation: "Nothing is more conducive to health and longevity than frequent household cleansings."

[4] A popular remedy of the day.

[5] Chalybeate waters, also known as ferruginous waters, are mineral spring waters containing salts of iron.

[6] Green vitriol, or ferrous sulphate (iron).

[7] Anise is a flowering plant, its seeds often ground up and used for teas and tinctures.

Rules of Health

but use a little wine for thy stomach's sake" (1 Tim. 5:23). And yet I would say, upon drinking a glass of generous wine, often take a glass of water. And if the beer they bring you be too strong, dilute it with putting a sufficient quantity of water into it. But never take water or anything else cold when you are hot with labor. There is death in the pot.

When you have run the hazard of disturbing your stomach with ingurgitations from a full table, a draught of cold water will do good like a medicine.

Going to bed and sweating from a large draught of cold water not only stops and cures a cold, but also often extinguishes a fever at the beginning.

Daily to wash your head and mouth with cold water is a practice that cannot be too much commended; if it were only for saving you from the toothache.

For a frequency in the use of the liquors, which they call "spirits," be as afraid of it as you would be of a familiarity with evil spirits.

VI. When you go to infectious places, one of the best things you can do is to hold and chew a bit of Myrrh in your mouth.

VII. To feed much on salt-meats won't be for your safety. Indeed, if less flesh were eaten, and more of the vegetable and farinaceous food were used, it were better. The milk-diet is for the most part some of the wholesomest in the world! And not the less wholesome for the coconut, giving a little tincture to it.

VIII. *Shall I smoke tobacco?* Answer: be sure, not if I can help it. Or let Alsted answer for me: *Maximus Tabaci Abusus est, quotidiano ejus usu, semetipsos, et bonas Horas perdere, et ex cerebro, mentis nobilissima sede, caminum et cloacam efficere.*[8] In the Dutchy of Berguen, people may not smoke without purchasing a license for it. If you were to purchase of me a license for it, I know not how high terms I should hold you to. If you want a hydragogue, there is one preferable in chewing some such thing as a bit of mastich; which would also whiten your teeth and sweeten your breath, which tobacco poisons. If once you get into the way of smoking, there will be extreme hazard of your becoming a slave to the pipe; and ever insatiably craving for it. People may think what they will; but such a slavery is much below the dignity of a rational creature; and much more of a gracious Christian. I am sure what the Great Voetius writes upon it is very true; *Minime convenit viris honest is et gravibus; nominatim Ministris et Ministerii Candidatis.*[9] There can be no apology for your taking up the slovenly practice, and the pains that must be taken to conquer the poison if you are not well advised and assured that your health requires it. But I shall only recite what you will find in two very considerable writers that you may form the better judgment upon it. The one of these writers is Magnenus, who though he be a mighty friend to the use of tobacco, yet acknowledges,

> That it is not easy to relate what are the damages which the inordinate and immoderate use of this

---

[8] Translation: "The greatest waste of tobacco is this, that by its daily use it destroys the users and the best of their lives (lit., "good seasons") and it brings forth from the brain, that most noble seat of reason, smoke and filth." (The translator's great-grandmother used to say she didn't smoke because she did not want the inside of her lungs to look like an ashtray).

[9] Translation: "It by no means agrees with honorable and serious men, especially ministers and candidates for the ministry."

Rules of Health

> fume does bring with it. For besides the insatiable and greedy lust of taking it, by its daily use, the memory is impaired, the stomach violated, the brain exiccated, and the life shortened; and the offspring damnified.

Yea, he lays this down as an undoubted assertion, that the frequent and familiar use of it can be good for no man. The other is our Gale, who from his own experience taxes the smoke of tobacco with very noxious qualities: He says,

> He found it made more humors than it brought away; and tho' it opened his body for the present, it proved in that very thing a prejudice afterwards; and nature was but the more sluggish and feeble anon, for the force in this way put upon it.

He says, "At last I came under a fixed resolution to deliver myself from this vassalage." And this I account not the least deliverance of my life. And yet, after all, I am not so inflexibly set, as utterly to deny you the use of tobacco, if you are sure of any benefit from it.

Only I insist upon it, that you be (If I may use a phrase that, if it may seem to trespass upon good sense, it shall yet have as much as the thing I write against) excessively moderate in it. And if you are growing so wise as to retrench and reform any intemperance in it, which you may have been unawares drawn into, do it not at once, but by degrees, lest by too quick a stop to an usual discharge, your health may be endangered. But, upon the whole, if you have hitherto escaped this epidemical contagion, and are not yet a settled inhabitant of the Terra del Fuogo, I cannot advise you in better terms than those; it is

Directions for a Candidate of the Ministry

good for you to abide even as you are. And, if you may be kept free, choose it rather. Yea, my son, if Smokers entice thee, consent thou not. It is good advice; and if you take it, you will one day thank him that gave it.

But if I am against your taking tobacco in smoke, you may be sure, I shall not approve your taking it in snuff. How shameful a thing it is for people of reason to confess that they can't live easily half an hour together without a delight so sensual, so trivial, so very contemptible, as that of tickling their olfactory nerves a little? And even bury themselves alive in pungent grains of titillating dust? A learned physician of the French nation will tell you how many diseases of the *Genus Nervosum* do issue out of that Pandora's Box from whence the pinch of snuff is taken. A Quincy will tell you how wretchedly it spoils the appetite. And a Cheyne will tell you how much the eyes, as well as the stomach, fare the worse for it. You may dream that the passage thro' the *Os Cribriforme* will not permit the gross powder of your snuff to enter into your brain; yet some very thin and fine parts of it will find their way thither. And what mischiefs must needs follow a brain so poisoned? Nay, one would think that the great snuff-takers had their brain already touched; or they could not be so obstinately and incurably attached unto an evil habit, which their folly has brought upon them. A very just motto for the snuff-box might be, "A leader to the coffin." If it be offered you, away with it! I say again, away with it!

IX. A knight of my acquaintance visiting the famous Dr. Lower in his last sickness asked him for the best advice he could give him; how to preserve his health, and prolong his life; the doctor only answered him: "Don't eat too much!" After some other discourse, the knight not imagining that the doctor had thoroughly answered his inquiry repeated it. The doctor thereupon only repeated his answer: "Why, didn't I tell you; don't eat too much!"—and further said not.

Sir Theodore Mayern on his deathbed gave this advice to a noble friend that asked his counsel for the preservation of his health. "Be moderate in your diet; use much exercise, and little physic." I would have added, guard against injurious changes of the weather; and especially be exposed unto the night-airs as little as may be.

X. Baglivi is not the only Gentleman who has observed how much tranquility and serenity of the mind contributes unto the health. Hofman, in his treatise, *Des Moyens de vivre Longtemps*, has observed, "That in the way of keeping the mind quiet, the fear of the Lord tends unto life. A holy and an easy mind is the most healthful thing under heaven." The most potent prophylactic in all the world, I need say no more.

Only this: forever *Obsta Principijs*.[10]—if any sickness come upon you, be sure to be sick soon enough. Maladies taken at the beginning may be easily and presently conquered; when—delays are dangerous. And if you are upon a recovery from any malady, Ben't well too soon.

---

[10] Translation: "Stand firm at the beginning."

20
RULES & MAXIMS
OF PRUDENCE

I have now no more to do, but only single out a few *rules of prudence*, the observation whereof may be your preservation from very many wrong steps in the way you have now before you. It cost the Prussians the trouble of a war before they could oblige their neighbors to call them no longer "Brutos," which they did before the tenth century, but "Prusses," which signifies, it seems, "A Prudent People." I wish it may cost you no more trouble than only a little reading of and thinking on certain maxims of prudence to render you one of that people. I shall not say how much it has cost me, and what a dear-bought experience it is that has enabled me to recommend them.

I will first suppose that you take that course of piety, "If any lack wisdom, let him ask it of God" (Jas. 1:5); and that you study the book of the Proverbs, which our Bible is enriched withal. I will also wish you to read the Lord Verulam's *Essays*. And I will mind you that one has lately written a book to show that wisdom lies in the not doing that which may any way prejudice human society, of which we are a part, but on the contrary make all our actions tend to the benefit of it. Then, I will offer you such hints as these:

I. The Italian maxims are no imprudent ones. One must not spend all he hath; nor do all he can; nor tell all he knows;

nor believe all he hears. And there is a sentence of a Greek poet worthy to be remembered with you; which in plain English will tell you, "No wise man will be taken a second time in an error he hath suffered for."

II. It is a lesson worth more than an ingott of gold, which one who saw many things has left for what is to be uttered in company; *Bis prius ad Limam quam semel ad Linguam.*[1] Think before you speak; think before whom you speak; think why as well as what you speak. And remember, *In multiloquio Stultiloquium*;[2] And least said soonest mended.

It is a very prudent remark. If one observes these three small imperatives, *Audi, Cerne, Tace,*[3] he will need no other passport for travelling over the world. You will have a good note of wisdom with two satellites to it in my reciting to you the observations of a very discrete man who said: "He had often got hurt by eating too much; rarely, by eating too little; often got hurt by wearing too few clothes; rarely, by wearing too many. Often got hurt by speaking; rarely, by holding his tongue."

III. You find Homer assigning that as the reason which made his Patroclus to be universally lamented at his death, he knew how to be good-natured unto all men. You may come to be almost universally beloved while you live, if your good nature (and good humor; what no nation or language but ours has a proper term for!), appear in continual demonstrations, which will satisfy everyone; that you shall delight in doing all good offices which they can desire of you; and that, if you see or hear

---

[1] Translation: "Thinks twice before speaking" (lit., "Twice to the file before once to the tongue").

[2] Translation: "In much speech is folly."

[3] Translation: "Listen, observe, be quiet."

anything disreputable in them, you will generously cast and keep a mantle over it.

IV. I have heard one say that there was a gentleman in the nineteenth chapter of the Acts, to whom he was more indebted than to any man in the world. This was he whom our translation calls the town-clerk of Ephesus; whose counsel it was to do nothing rashly. Upon any proposal of consequence, it was a usual speech with him. We'll first advise with the town-clerk of Ephesus. One in a fond compliance with a friend, forgetting the town-clerk, may do that in haste which he may repent at leisure; may do what may cost him several hundreds of pounds, besides troubles which he would not have undergone for thousands.

V. Let the Judges motto be yours, *Prudens qui Patiens*.[4] You will forever find "the wrath of man works not the righteousness of God" (Jas. 1:20). And there is nothing done so well in a passion, but what may be done better out of it. There is a conspicuous wisdom in meekness. If you find your spirit heated in discourse at any time—now, now is a time for the bridle: "I will take heed to my ways that I sin not with my tongue." There is danger lest a Moses himself speak unadvisedly with his lips when his anger is moved. Suppress rather than express too warm resentments, whatever be the provocations. There will be nothing lost by doing so—*Motos praestat componere fluctus*.[5]

VI. If you feel a violent impulse hurrying you into an eager pursuit of any matter, be jealous, be afraid, lest you be led into temptation. Examine it over and over again; and be upon a

---

[4] Translation: "Patience is prudence." (lit., "He who is patient is also prudent").

[5] Translation: "Better to calm the tossing waves." Vergil, *Aeneid* 1.135.

most sedate weighing of the matter, well-assured that it is what will not be repented of.

VII. Let it be as a law of the Medes and Persians with you, that you will never sacrifice any hours of a short life in contentions; especially in personal contentions and quarrels and squabbles and vitilitigations.[6] Abundance of sin will be unavoidably committed in them; and the game will not pay for the candle. Remit rather of much right, which you may have a claim unto than contend for it. This is the meaning of, "Let your moderation be known unto all men" (Phil. 4:5). In using an uncommon lenity and forbearance, and condescension, under unfair usages, you will find the Lord u at hand; ready in strange ways to make you reparation for the wrongs that men may have done you. Yea, why may you not look on the peace you purchase by it as a sufficient reparation?

VIII. Sometimes a vindication may be necessary. In what cases—wisdom will be profitable to direct you. But if it be, at any time, whispered unto you that any one has despised you, derided you, spoken diminutively of you; the best way, for the most part is for you to take no more notice of it than a greater man (a Theodosius) would have done of such a contempt cast upon him. Let them that have abused you know nothing that you know anything of the matter. For such is the baseness of many people, that (measuring you by themselves) they will hate you, because you know that they have hurt you; and they will persist in their hatred, which they must justify, because they imagine that you can't forgive them. Whereas, if you be silent, and as one that hears not, God will probably reward your

---

[6] Contention, backbiting.

patient silence by making those very persons anon prove some of the most cordial and useful friends you have in the world.

IX. Don't use your pen and lose your time in eristic writings, any more than unquestionable duty and prudence makes to be absolutely necessary. Writing upon a point, and in the way and strain of controversy, will not only have a tendency to discompose the peace of your mind, but miserably divert the studies of a short pilgrimage from such things as would be much more profitable for yourself and others. Anon, the grand point of the controversy will be, only who has most wit or grace of the two—you or your antagonist. A mighty business! If Jerome were pleased in a hectoring way to forewarn his opponents, that he was, *Cornuta Bestia*;[7] I hope you won't be so.

X. If calumnious quills have publicly scratched you—*An Respondendum semper Calumniis?*[8]—no. Look as far back as two thousand years ago, and you will find even a Plato giving a pattern to a Christian in his declining to take any notice of the invectives which a Xenophon had used upon him. It may be the scribblers are sorry scoundrels, and such vile children of Sheth, as it is beneath you to let them know that you have so much as read their follies. Or be they what they will, for the most part, the best way will be to shine on, regardless of what the bats and owls may mutter against you. Or, if that metaphor be too sublime, let me say, at least as the moon among the lesser fires keep a steady pace, walking in your brightness, notwithstanding the unregardable allatrations of your adversaries. If they persecute you with libels, 'tis a notable hint that Le Clero has given you. Instead of answering them, write such learned and useful books as will be of perpetual service to mankind. These will procure

---

[7] Translation: "A horned beast."

[8] Translation: "Should you always respond with calumny?"

Directions for a Candidate of the Ministry

such a casting and lasting testimony for you that there will need no more to make a man ill thought of than this; that he was a Thersites to you, and one that wrote against you. These books will be durable monuments of your valuable and honorable character, when the libels of these poor Animalculicuncles[9] will perish among the waste-paper, which the haberdashers of small wares have occasion for.

And if any preacher should be so impertinent as to have any girds at you in the pulpit, remember the advice of the sweet-spirited Melanchthon to Vitus Theodorus, when the hot-spirited Osiander had preached against him; "I charge you, don't answer the man. Hold your peace; go on in your ministry as if you had heard nothing!"—the gentleman soon found his account in hearkening to his candid adviser.

That what I am driving may stick, you shall have it in the form of two old rusty nails; the one, *Magnum Contumeliae Remedium Negligentia*;[10] The other, *Sile, et funestam dedisti Plagam*.[11]

As wicked a fellow as ever polluted a pen, yet has this passage worth transcribing from him, while his name is not worth mentioning.

> The malice of ill tongues cast upon a good man is only like a mouthful of smoke blown upon a diamond, which tho' it clouds its beauty for the present, yet it is easily rubbed off, and the gem restored with little trouble to its genuine luster.

---

[9] A microscopic organism.
[10] Translation: "Ignoring it is the great remedy for reproach."
[11] Translation: "Be silent, and you have given the death stroke."

But an honester pagan than he has told you, *Perditi Hominis profligatique Maledictis, nullius Gloria dignitas {que} Violatur.*[12] Old Cicero tells you so.

XI. Be sociable. But throw away as little time as ever you can upon the *Temporis Fures*;[13] especially upon impertinent company. Keep company, but let it be chiefly with such as are your superiors; your familiarity with whom will be reputable and serviceable to you.

XII. While you are yet in your younger years, be always furnished with a stock of weighty and useful questions. By wisely and humbly offering these, and with the modesty of one desiring to be instructed, you may commonly lead the conversation, even with your superiors, and almost necessitate a profitable conversation. You may be, as R. Jeremy was called, "The Master of the Questions." A discretion in this point is a distinguishing thing. But whenever you are arguing, ordinarily propose everything rather Socratically than dogmatically. Be not positive; much less clamorous; least of all furious. But keep up an air of modesty, and carry on your discourse in the form of proper questions; and as one willing to be instructed by him whom you are disputing with. 'Tis an excellent wisdom, this: to argue handsomely.

XIII. Find out some very wise and some very good person whom you may choose to make, what we call, "A Bosom Friend." But be very careful of your choice; for, "A faithful friend, who can find?" When you have such a one, ask his advice in all matters of importance. Nevertheless, even here,

---

[12] Translation: "By the curses of a wicked and profligate man the reputation and dignity of no one is violated." Cicero, *De Haruspicum Responso* 22.46.

[13] Translation: "Thieves of time."

keep your stops as to trusting him with such secrets as may put it into his power to hurt you. At least, rarely commit any secrets to any persons, but such as may have it as much for their interest as it is for yours, to keep them so.

XIV. Lay hands suddenly on no man! There is in the wisdom of the Ancients, a caution against blessing a friend with a loud voice, rising early in the morning. There is a marvelous wisdom as well as goodness in speaking well of everyone, as far as we can, on all occasions, and even watching for all occasions to do so. And evil-speaking has an indiscretion as well as indecency in it; for the very birds of the air strangely report the matter. But yet there is often a want of wisdom in our being either too copious or too early in our commendations: too high or too quick. You may sooner than you think for, see your commendations confuted; and be obliged (as even Calvin once) to revoke your dedications. *Qualem commendes etiam at {que} etiam aspice.*[14]

XV. Let no man of quality engage you, and attach you so far to his interests, that you shall run the hazard of abating the success of your ministry, and abridging your opportunities to do good unto many upon his account. You will find such men, what the Oracles of God foretell you shall, when you put your trust in them. They will soon fall out with you if you don't keep touch with them in all their designs; and when you cease to be their tool, they will most forgetfully and ungratefully abandon you. Nor will it be wisdom in you to go any further in appearing for any government (As the world now goes!) than duty calls you to it. If you do, I can tell, how you shall be requited for it! If any factions arising in the Commonwealth solicit your

---

[14] Translation: "Examine over and over what sort of person it is that you recommend." Horace, *Epistles* 18.

embarcation in them, keep close to the business of your ministry, and say, "I am doing a great work, so that I cannot come down. Why should the work cease, while I leave it, and come down to you?" To be a State-Martyr, 'tis what I can't advise you to be ambitious of. I have nothing to say for such a crown of martyrdom. Yet thus much I insist upon. Be sure to keep forever loyal and faithful to the Protestant line, for the British scepter.

XVI. Gain by everything! Let reproaches make you consider, "To what excellent virtue and action would He that has bidden this to befall me thereby awaken me?" Yea, let all disasters make you consider, "What admonition does my God now send unto me?"

XVII. If you have laid up an inexhaustible store of stories accommodated unto all the purposes of the profitable and the agreeable, and have the skill of telling them handsomely, and with a deliberate, expressive, unstumbling brevity, and produce them on many occasions, you may not only ingratiate yourself wherever you make your appearance, but also obtain almost any request that you shall make one of them a witty introduction to. The precious stones that everyone sets a value on are called "Pleasant Stones." But let not your pleasancy degenerate into any unbecoming levity. Forever so regulate it, and so moderate it, that it may gracefully terminate in the most serious discourse, and if it may be, in the inculcation and insinuation of some serious maxim, which may be good for the use of edifying.

XVIII. In public transactions, and especially when anything is driving about which the people of God may be divided in their sentiments, let there be a continual terror of God upon you, lest you unawares fall in with something that may be inimical or detrimental to the Kingdom of God; continually suspicious, lest some stratagem of Satan may draw you into something that may gratify that Great Adversary. For example, things may look very plausibly, and there may seem a laudable regard paid unto peace, and love, and charity in them; and yet it may be a prostituted charity, which going so far as to embrace those for brethren in Christ who are enemies to Him, it may prove a treachery to the most glorious cause in the world. And so, there was once in the low countries that pressed under the name of *moderation*, which others found and called, *murderation*.

Be very thoughtful, and very prayerful on such occasions.

XIX. It may not be amiss for you to have two heaps. A heap of unintelligibles; and a heap of incurables. Every now and then you will meet with something or other that may pretty much distress your thoughts; but the shortest way with the vexations will be to throw them into the heap they belong to, and be no more distressed about them.

You will meet with some unaccountable and incomprehensible things; particularly, in the conduct of many people. Throw them into your heap of *unintelligibles*; leave them there. Trouble your mind no further; hope the best, or think no more about them.

You will meet with some unpersuadable people. No counsel, no reason will do anything upon the obstinates; especially as to the making of due submissions upon offenses. Throw them into the heap of *incurables*. Leave them there. And so do you go on to do as well as you can, what you have to do. Let not the crooked things that can't be made straight encumber you.

XX. 'Tis a trespass on the rules of prudence never to know when to have done. Wherefore, I have done!

PRUDENCE

And now, go thy way, O thou son greatly beloved; and work in thy lot livelily, and prayerfully, and cheerfully to the end of thy days; and wait and look for what the Glorious Lord will do for thee at the end of thy days; in those endless joys, wherein thou shalt shine as the brightness of the firmament, and as the stars forever and ever.

Audendum est, ut illustratr Veritus Tatea, multique ab Errore Liberentur. Lactant.[15]

---

[15] Translation: "It must be dared, in order that the truth of the Father might be illustrated, and many freed from error. Let them have milk."

A CATALOGUE OF BOOKS
for a Young Student's Library

- Bailey's *English Dictionary*.
- Ward's *Introduction to the Mathematicks*.
- Kennet's, *Roman Antiquities*.
- Potter's, *Archeologia Attica*.
- Lewis's *Origines Hebraeae*.
- Gordon's *Geographical Grammar*.
- Wells's, *Sacred Geography*.
- Mat. Prideaux, his *Introduction for Reading all Sorts of History*.
- Whiston's *Chronology*.
- Spanheim, his *Introductio ad Historiam Sacram*
- *The Christian Philosopher*.
- Whitlock's, *Memorials*, both volumes.
- Fuller's *Worthies of England*.
- Leigh, his *Critica Sacra*, both parts.
- Charnock's *Works*.
- Poole's *Annotations*.
- Strong, *On the Covenant*.
- Polhil, his *Speculum Theologiae in Christo*.
- The Leyden, *Synopsis Purioris Theologiae*.
- Maestricht, his *Theologia Theoretico-practica*.
- Ravenellus, his *Bibliotheca*.
- Edwards, his *Preacher*.
- And, *Theologia Reformata*.
- Arndt, his *Verus Christianismus*.
- The Common-Place Book to the Holy Scriptures.

For Further Reading:

Kennedy, Rick. *The First American Evangelical: A Short Life of Cotton Mather*. Grand Rapids: Eerdmans, 2015.

Levin, David. *Cotton Mather: The Young Life of the Lord's Remembrancer, 1663-1703*. Cambridge: Harvard University Press, 1978.

Lovelace, Richard. *The American Pietism of Cotton Mather: Origins of American Evangelicalism*. Grand Rapids: Eerdmans, 1979.

Middlekauff, Robert. *The Mathers: Three Generations of Puritan Intellectuals, 1596-1728*. Berkeley: University of California Press, 1999.

Miller, Perry. *The New England Mind: From Colony to Province*. Cambridge: Harvard University Press, 1953.

Ryken, Leland. *Worldly Saints: The Puritans As They Really Were*. Grand Rapids: Zondervan, 1990.

Silverman, Kenneth. *The Life and Times of Cotton Mather*. New York: Welcome Rain Publishers, 1984.

Smolinski, Reiner and Steivermann, Jan, eds. *Cotton Mather and Biblia Americana—America's First Bible Commentary: Essays in Reappraisal*. Grand Rapids: Baker Academic, 2010.

Scripture Index

New Testament

John		Philippians	
12:26	107	4:5	156
Romans		1 Timothy	
2:15	10	5:23	147
5:19	109	James	
12:21	126	1:5	153
1 Corinthians		1:20	155
2:2	105	2 Peter	
14:10–11	116	1:7	138
		Revelation	
		4:6	xxi

Name	Date Read

www.ingramcontent.com/pod-product-compliance
Lightning Source LLC
Chambersburg PA
CBHW021442070526
44577CB00002B/257